Chewing, Tugg
Biting:

Detailed Step-by-Step Training for Puppies and Dogs

By Faye Dunningham

Preface

When you have a puppy or dog, any issues of chewing, tugging, nipping or biting can take a "bite" out of the fun of ownership! While every puppy is adorable and cute, often their behavior can be "not so cute".

For each issue, we will be discussing all of the possible causes so that you can handle things in an exact way depending on how and why your puppy or dog is behaving as his is.

Training for chewing, tugging, nipping and/or biting is crucial. One must remember that any behavior such as this can continue on for life if an owner does not step in. For example, a teething puppy may display destructive behavior as he chews up everything in his path; while the chewing was *initially* caused by the discomfort of teething, if the puppy is not shown that his behavior is unacceptable, he may then continue on as a "chewer" for the rest of his life.

This can be said for nipping as well. Most puppies will nip based on instinctual canine behavior that began as young as three weeks old. If this is not handled properly, a puppy will often not outgrow this. Without proper guidance, a puppy can be a "nipper" for life.

There are *other* puppies that will nip as a method of saying, *"Leave me alone!"* and this can be shocking and heartbreaking to an owner. "Where is that cute little puppy that I wanted so badly?" these owners will think. If a puppy nips and it is clearly *not* intended as part of "play", this is undoubtedly a case of a puppy *not* perceiving their owner as the leader. In this case, specific training will be implemented.

Most important is that an owner teaches a puppy using methods that the puppy will understand. We will discuss how to first create an atmosphere that allows your puppy to understand you…And then exactly how to go about shaping his behavior from negative to positive.

With your goal of having a peaceful, happy household, it is imperative to show your puppy what is acceptable and what is not acceptable. This does not need to be done with an iron fist and doing so can actually make things worse. These methods are incorporated in a loving way. When training for this is done correctly, it is carried through without "tapping" the dog and without yelling.

In order for a dog to learn that certain behaviors are not acceptable, an owner must be seen as the leader. Yet he or she can be a ***very*** just and loving leader. The puppy will be corrected with fair-mindedness… and this type of guidance will then encourage the puppy to develop into an extremely well-behaved, well-mannered dog.

While you are reading this book, once you reach the training sections you may wish to rush right in and start teaching your puppy or dog. Since this book will give you detailed training for just about every type of situation regarding chewing, tugging, nipping and biting, it is suggested that you read through the entire book first. Then, you can go back to choose which training methods best fit your specific needs.

Enjoy your read!

Table of Contents

The "Why's" of Chewing, Tugging, Nipping and Biting

Cause and Trigger

Just about every owner of a puppy will deal with chewing, tugging, nipping and/or biting issues. These can be separate and distinct issues, each with their own cause and trigger. In other words, each is caused by a certain reason and each will need to be dealt with independently from the others with specific training.

Alternatively, some or all of them, can be connected. In other words, a puppy that is chewing, tugging, nipping and biting may be doing all of these things for the same basic reason, and training will encompass this far-reaching behavioral trigger to work on all issues simultaneously.

If this behavior is not properly handled by you, the owner, it can carry on throughout adolescence and into adulthood.

What one must remember is that while canines are intelligent, they do not automatically create a long thought process of: intention, action and reaction. While humans usually think things through, dogs often make fast decisions based on instinct. Luckily, while "intention" will remain, a dog's actions and reactions can be shaped by the owner.

The ultimate goal of this training is for a dog to pause in order to have the "action and reaction" thoughts...after training is complete and reinforced, your dog will automatically react in the positive way that you desire, without much thought at all. It will become natural for him to behave nicely.

When a human thinks about an idea, they may consider all possible outcomes and once they decide that it is in their favor to do any particular action they may then proceed to do so. Once the action is taken, there is a result. A person, often thinking in their own best interest, will then decide if they did indeed gain something or if the action/behavior was actually detrimental. Our puppies and dogs can learn this valuable and beneficial way of thinking before taking action.

Chewing, tugging, nipping and biting can be the resulting actions of various triggers, however the two main reasons are: instinct and attention. To understand that this behavior is often due to instinct is very important so that an owner begins this training with the right mindset. Often a puppy will be labeled as "bad" because he chews, tugs, nips and/or bites. However, this is not true. While the behavior itself may be seen as "bad" and certainly it is a negative behavior, this does not mean that the puppy itself is bad.

Remember that puppies must be taught and shown what is appropriate and acceptable and what is not. As owners, we are asking *canines* to live in a *human's* world and to conform to what *we* consider to be appropriate behavior, which is often in opposition to canine instinct.

These are lessons that owners must take time to instill and our pets should never be expected to figure this out on their own. Additionally, unless training is done in a way that a canine understands, all of the begging, pleading, yelling and/or frustrations that an owner sends out will be ineffective.

Expecting an adorable and cute puppy to have the same behavior as their appearance suggests is normal. When a puppy displays chewing, nipping and other negative behaviors, this can be shocking and frustrating. Some owners worry that they made a mistake in obtaining the dog… or wonder if the pup somehow has a flawed personality.

This type of thinking can cause an owner to react under duress, responding in a way that actually encourages the behavior. When this happens, words and actions are perceived by their puppy in a way that the owner did not intend.

This then creates a vicious cycle: the puppy nips, he does not understand that it was an unacceptable behavior, the puppy nips again, the owner is frustrated and does not change his method of dealing with it, the puppy nips again and so on.

A Puppy's Interactions and Explorations

When we talk about instinct, some of these behaviors begin long before you ever bring your puppy home. They can begin at the age of 3 weeks old. A newborn is born with his eyes closed and with no teeth. He has very limited control over his bowels, if at all. All that he knows at this time is the feel of comfort (being close to the dam and enjoying her warmth) and the need to fill his empty stomach. The first few weeks are a time of intense sleeping and almost continual nourishment.

There are incredible changes by the 3 week mark. Eye lids that once remained closed have now gradually opened and sight is coming into focus. Able to see, a whole new world opens up to him. While he once scooted over to his mother, he is now learning to walk. After he finds his gait (wobbly at first but soon trotting around), he is able to explore his surroundings. While he had a sense of his littermates, he is now able to intentionally and physically interact with them. He is able to play with them. He is able to socialize with them in a very basic way.

One of the very first things that puppies will do to interact with their new world is to use their mouth. Since puppies, of course, do not have opposable thumbs, they learn with their mouths. Their mouth tells them what something is. They discover which elements are foods and which are not. They use their mouths to pick things up; they will then either drop it, keep the object to chew on or carry it to another location. One of the most important things that a puppy will do with his mouth is to use it in play. And this is where the habits and behaviors of chewing, tugging, nipping and biting are born.

During the ages of 3 weeks old to approximately 6 weeks old, the world of a puppy is limited. While it is new to him and he is very excited about exploring it, he must still remain close to the dam for nourishment and be enclosed for safety reasons. Therefore, the one element that becomes his biggest "plaything" is his brothers and sisters.

 Canine litter size varies greatly...Chihuahuas will have small litters of 1-3 pups...Litters from Labrador Retrievers range in size from 5-10. The largest litter recorded was 24 puppies (with 20 surviving) born to a Mastiff.

Instinctual play begins at this very young age. If you have ever had the opportunity to watch 3, 4 and 5 week old newborns at play you would see them rolling all over each other. You would see them crawling on top of each other and notably, you would see them mouthing and biting each other.

Something occurs at this very young age. It is one of the very first life lessons that a puppy learns. Unfortunately, it is often soon forgotten once he leaves the litter to go to his new home. During this brief time of a few weeks, he learns that nipping and biting is not acceptable. He learns this from his littermates and in some cases he will also learn this lesson from the dam.

When a puppy nips and bites at his brother or sister and does so with enough force to cause discomfort, he is told in no uncertain terms that the action will not be tolerated. The "victim" lets out a yelp that is often quite loud. The "victim" will then refuse to play with the offender.

In some cases, the dam will step in. She is bound by instinct to protect her entire litter and upon seeing a potential or real injury to one of her pups; she will often step in to shove away the offender. He is now being ignored by his brother or sister and quite possibility he has also been isolated by his mother. Now what is he to do? All that he wants to do is to play. That enjoyment is taken away from him, even if only for a short time.

In most cases, he will wait anywhere from 10 seconds to 2 minutes and then jump back into the fray. And then something happens. As his mouth opens to bite at a littermate, he will think about that for a moment. This short but important time of thinking about the repercussion of his intention may happen after one incident of biting too hard as described earlier or it may happen on time number ten. However, when it does occur, the puppy has learned one of his very first lessons.

He has learned that his actions equal consequences. He now has a fast decision to make: Does he go with instinct to nip or bite or does the unhappy idea of hearing that yelp and being ignored outweigh his instinct? Making a decision based on what is most beneficial to him, the puppy chooses to not nip or bite, or at the very least he will do so in a much gentler way as to not produce any negative consequences.

Your Job as a Loving Owner

It would be wonderful if this lesson stayed with a puppy. It would be much easier for owners to raise a puppy (or an older, adopted dog) if this lesson was instilled in the dog's mind and ruled his behavior for life. However, much will soon change and this lesson will  be forgotten. The behavior of chewing, tugging, nipping and biting will emerge in full force for the owner to deal with. Gone are the teachings of his littermates and gone are the teachings of his mother. For this training, you will be re-teaching this lesson to your puppy.

You, the owner, are now not only responsible for the health and well-being of your puppy; you are also responsible for his behavior. As a loving owner it is you who must teach many lessons to your puppy.

You will teach him about the world. You will show him how to safely walk next to you. You will teach him how to interact with other people and with other animals. And importantly, you will teach him that chewing on anything other than approved toys, tugging at you or your clothes, and nipping and biting at you or any other person is not appropriate behavior.

But, why should your puppy listen to you? *You* know that you are the owner. Chances are that you spent a good deal of money to obtain your puppy or you searched high and low for just the right dog to adopt. But, does your puppy know that? Your puppy or dog knows that you are not a canine. He may not have a detailed understanding of what a "human" is, but he does know that you are of a different species. He is aware that you are taller. He is aware that you are a presence in his life. However, this is not enough for him to follow your guidance.

The key element to training any puppy or dog to stop chewing, tugging, nipping and/or biting is to purposely and steadfastly show him that you are not just a human in his life, you are the leader. If he does not have a solid and complete understanding of this, he has no reason or inclination to follow your orders, care what you think or have reason to be concerned with what you may or may not consider to be inappropriate behavior.

We will discuss this very important element in the following chapter.

The First Things You Must Do

How a Dog Perceives His Owner

You can use the correct tone of voice for training, you can follow all of the steps perfectly and you can train each day. All of these elements have one thing in common: A puppy will *not* give weight to an owner's message unless he sees his owner as his leader.

Some owners think that a dog will *naturally* assume that the human is the leader; however this often is not true. It is easy to think that this should be a "given". After all, you put thought into bringing a dog into your household. You wanted not only a pet but most likely you envisioned having a best friend and canine family member.

Maybe you spent countless hours on the computer searching for just the right breeder. Maybe you spent your weekends searching through shelters for just the right puppy to adopt. You may have even gotten your puppy or dog on a whim because it just "felt right".

No matter what the process was that someone obtained a puppy or dog and no matter how much money was or was not spent, an owner is not a "leader" unless they make this clear to a dog.

Your puppy or dog does not understand the terminology of "owner". What canines *do* understand is the feeling of being in a "pack". And they know, by instinct, that every pack has a leader. There is a good chance that you have heard about this concept; however many owners believe that just by the fact that they are the taller, more intelligent species that this means that they are obviously perceived as the leader. If it were that easy, training would be wrapped up in one day and all dogs would behave perfectly.

The fact is that a dog knows that he is in a pack, whether this be just the two of you or a mixture of ten people and other household pets. One of the most common problems is that the element of "who is the leader?" of that pack may be undefined. That is not a good thing, since it can cause inner turmoil as a canine struggles to figure out his place.

In other cases, the element of "who's the leader?" can be misinterpreted by puppies and dogs. They may think (usually by being unintentionally encouraged) that they are the leader. They may even think that another household pet is the leader. In some cases, a puppy or dog may have been given the impression that one particular person in the house is the leader and that all other humans are at or below that rank.

When a puppy or dog does not have a clear strong understanding of "who's the leader?" this causes many problems. One of the main problems will be negative behavior such as chewing, tugging, nipping and biting. Why? Without leadership your dog is on his own. Yes... You feed him, you buy him toys, you bring him to the veterinarian and you do so many things for him. However, this does not establish you as the leader.

When without leadership, a puppy or dog will do one of two things: He will take the role of leader or he will struggle and "fight" for that role with other humans or pets in the home. The struggle will go on forever if the issue is never settled. When this is the case, chaos can become the norm and that, of course, does not make for peaceful happy home.

When a puppy or dog thinks that he is the leader, he will do as he sees fit, since he has no boundaries. Any yelling or pleading for his behavior to change will be disregarded. Any training will be ignored. Some owners, out of frustration, tap a puppy that is nipping. Tapping a puppy on the bottom or on the muzzle does no good and can actually cause a dog to become more aggressive since he is being "tapped" by someone whom he perceives to be equal or below him in rank.

A dog that does not see you as leader may love you, but he often will not listen to you. He may come to you when called and he will enjoy a good tummy rub. But when it comes down to behavior, if he believes that he is in charge, he will chew, nip and bite as he pleases.

Showing Leadership Qualities in a Loving Way

So, how do you establish yourself as the leader? How do you make it clear to your dog that you are in charge? Luckily, all owners *are* capable of doing this. One of the most important elements needed is consistency. If you show leadership qualities one day, but fail to do so that next day, all that you will be doing is confusing your dog. If he is undecided about who is the leader or if he has a false belief about who is the "Alpha" (another terminology used for "leader") then he is confused enough!

Being a leader does not mean that you will be giving orders all day long. It does not mean that you need to be serious all of the time; nor does it mean that you cannot be your dog's best friend. When you are the leader, you can be the kindest, most caring and loving leader possible. However, you will not tolerate any behavior that you reasonably deem to be undesirable.

It will be your job to continue to provide excellent care for your dog. You will feed him well and make sure that he enjoys proper exercise. You will cuddle with your dog when you are feeling down and you will hug him when you receive good news. He will be your faithful friend and companion for life. So, do not allow the term of "leader" to mean anything other than the person who protects and guides a dog.

When a dog does not have a clear understanding or he has a wrong understanding of leadership, he is at his core, not happy. As a caring owner, you want your dog to be as happy as possible! A dog that does not have clear leadership in his life is a dog without a proper pack. Instinct, strong and inbred for thousands of years, impacts your dog every day. Dogs desire, crave, and only feel safe and secure when in a well-run pack (the people and other pets that they live with).

Their pack is their world. It holds things together. It offers structure. While all puppies and dogs have minds of their own, of course, they need for things to make sense. Living in a "pack" and having a leader be in charge of that pack makes sense to a dog. Once things are in order and you have established yourself as being in charge, your dog will relax.

If it was unclear to him exactly who was in charge, he can let go of the struggle of trying to figure it out. If he took on the position of leader, he can unwind as he will no longer feel the weight of that responsibility. Therefore, while you are keeping in mind that you will be a very loving leader, also remember that you will be making changes to ensure that your dog is happy.

You may think that this section does not apply to you. However, if your puppy or dog chews on anything other than toys, tugs at your clothes and/or nips and bites and you have tried to stop him from doing this, it means that he is not listening to you.

A dog always follows the orders of the leader (the Alpha). If he does listen, it will be because he considers himself to be the leader, fully capable of making his own decisions or it will be because he perceives a "weakness" in his owner and therefore desires to "fight" for the Alpha position. Following this train of thought, if your dog is not obeying your commands, it must be conceded that it is time to make a change and establish leadership. Only then will the training for chewing, tugging, nipping and biting work successfully.

We spoke a bit before about the need for being consistent; it is a vital key to all of this. So, let us recap that when you begin to do this it must be done in a serious way. It is a commitment that you will be making. You now know that your dog will be happier if you do this. You now know that once you do this that the training will work and that *you* will then be happier.

Therefore, go into this with firm affirmation that you will carry this through. Yes, life can be busy. You have a lot of things to do. However, it takes very little time to do this. With most of the steps, all that you will be doing is adjusting how things are done and not adding anything.

It may seem as if the steps that you will be taking do not seem so special. You may wonder why you should do them at all. Will it really make a difference? The answer is yes. To a canine, your actions mean a lot. If you are *not* seen as Alpha, your dog *constantly* assimilates your actions to see if you will continue to "agree" that *he* is the leader.

If you *are* seen as Alpha, your dog will forever look to your actions for any signs of "weakness"…As seeing weakness (a lax in leadership) causes canine instinct to take charge. That dog will then be on guard, ready to step in as leader if his instinct tells him that it is necessary in order for the "pack" to have an "Alpha".

With leadership either undefined or about to have a major change (if he sees himself as the leader) the small things that you will do are going to have a huge impact. So know that what you will be doing is very important.

Things will be a bit different depending on whether you are the only human in the home or if there are other family members. Things will also be different depending on if you have other pets. We will go over the various living situations that you may be in.

A Strong Statement

How you go about feeding your puppy or dog will have a great impact on how he perceives you. The method that you use will make a strong, clear statement that will affect whether he will or will not listen to you.

Only puppies under the age (in general) of 3 months old should be free-fed. That means that fresh food will be left out all day. It should be noted that some dog breeds *do* need food throughout the entire day but this is rare. Most toy sized, small, medium, large and giant breeds are ready to be put on a feeding schedule at some point during the puppy months, and this is typically by the age of 3 months at which time you will switch from free-feeding to 3 meals per day plus snacks.

Feeding time is a wonderful opportunity to show and instill the fact that you are the leader. Food is very important to dogs. They have a deep understanding that food is a huge, fundamental part of their survival. You, of course, understand that it takes very little effort to open a can of food or to scoop out some kibble and put it into a bowl. Even if you home cook for your puppy or dog, you most likely have the recipes down pat and it does not monopolize your time. But your dog does not know about this.

Your puppy or dog can become very impressed when having a full understanding that his meals come directly from you. It must be taught to a puppy that it is *entirely* up to you whether he eats or not. You will show him that he only eats if you, the leader, makes a clear decision that he does so.

Your dog must understand that the food bowl does not fill itself. If food is quickly placed down, a dog can assume that it "magically" got there and he will gobble it down without giving it a second thought. The goal here will be to take steps so that your puppy has no doubt that his food (his basic survival need) is offered to him from you (and any other humans who may live in the household).

When he learns this, he will have a deep respect for you. Done only once, it will have a very temporary impact. Done at every meal time and every time a treat is given it will have a *huge* impact. His respect for you will grow each day. His mind will form a stronger and stronger opinion about your place in the pack. When done along with the other key steps in establishing yourself as leader, he will have no choice. Canine instinct will dictate how you are perceived and in turn, how well your puppy or dog listens to you.

If you have more than one person living in the home, a schedule should be written up so that everyone takes a turn in offering food (both meals and snacks) to your dog. Problems can arise if only one person is assigned to this task; as a dog will often take this to mean that a *specific* person holds a higher rank than the other people in the home. This can create a situation where a dog may nip at everyone except the food provider.

If your puppy is on a schedule of 3 meals per day and you have 3 humans in the house, this will be easy to plan out. If you have 2 people, yet 3 feeding times, you can take turns: 1 person can provide breakfast and dinner while the other does lunch. The next day, you can switch. Therefore, depending on how many people are in your house you can create a routine that works for everyone.

 How much do dogs eat? Each meal will range from ¼ cup to a whopping 4 cups, depending on breed and age. How much does it cost to feed a dog for one year? The cost for toy breeds averages $120.00...with the cost for feeding large breed dogs averaging $400.00.

It is highly recommended to have children included in this as well. When supervised, children as young as five-years-old can give commands and offer food. Puppies and dogs often see children in one of two ways: Either as their equal or under them in terms of rank in the pack. When see as underlings, this is not a *terribly* negative aspect in regard to the fact that a dog who feels this way will often be very protective of "his" children.

When seeing a child as a *leader*, the dog *will* also protect as canines will protect regardless of rank. Behaving as a protector is a trait that will not go away once a child grows older. Canine instinct dictates that a dog will have a desire to protect all humans and the property that all of you live on.

So what is the *negative* aspect to having children seen as equals or underlings and why is it important to include youngsters in this training? As your puppy grows, so will your children. Time goes by quickly…The notion of a 5-year-old child who may be seen as an equal by a dog may seem "cute" however it will not seem so endearing when that child is 10-years-old and the dog that is now an adult will not obey their commands and may continue to nip, bark and perhaps even bite.

If you have an older dog and not a puppy, things will be a bit different. It is not uncommon for adult and especially senior dogs to have a low tolerance for children. The noises that children can make while at play and their high energy level can often cause an older dog to nip as a warning that basically means, "Keep your distance, I have no patience for your frolicking!"

However, when that adult or senior dog learns that the child actually holds a high position in the pack because that the child plays a part in deciding the dog's survival (by displaying leadership decisions such as feeding), the dog will then develop a respect. While a senior dog may not change enough that he rolls around with a child at play, he will no doubt simply retreat to a quieter place when he feels disturbed and nipping will end.

Therefore, the following method of feeding will be greatly beneficial in regard to a dog of any age, from an 8-week-old new puppy to a 12-year-old senior dog. Additionally, everyone in the home should be involved and all must be aware of the seriousness of how things will now be done. It is suggested to have a family meeting so that everyone can be on the same page. It is important that everyone understands the need to be consistent. Everyone will work as a team and this means that all are responsible the failure or success of this. Once all humans understand their task, choose a day and begin.

It should be noted that if you do not yet have one and only one designated feeding area, one should be chosen immediately. If you generally place the bowl down anywhere in the kitchen, this must change. Treats can be given anywhere (while following the methods we will talk about); however meals that are in your dog's bowl should be placed down in the same spot at all times.

It should be a quiet spot. Kitchens are often busy rooms. For many families it is a "meeting" area of sorts... While someone is cooking, a child may be doing their homework at the kitchen table and another person may be talking about how their day was.

Many owners are so accustomed to the normal activity in the kitchen; most don't think about trying to see it from a dog's point of view. However, dogs are very sensitive to where they eat. Even if it appears that your puppy wolfs down his food and is not paying attention to anything, he is actually very aware of what is happening.

He knows how close or how far away people are, he is aware of the tones of the voices that he hears, he knows if people are walking around and if anyone comes (to what he feels) is too close to his food. All of this is spinning through a dog's mind while he is eating. In some cases it will even be the direct cause of a dog quickly ingesting his meals; which can lead to stomach upset or in worst case scenarios, bloat.

Therefore, a corner of the kitchen that receives the smallest amount of foot traffic is best. The spot chosen should not be near a door where people will be entering and exiting while the dog eats. If there simply is not a quiet corner in your kitchen, you may even need to re-think which room you feed your dog in, however it must be situated so that the dog can see his human family eating.

A very vital component to this is that if a dog is given the message that a person is his leader (because the food was given to him in a specific way), but then that leader leaves him to "fend" for himself in regard to protecting the bowl until he has ingested all of the food, it will not have much weight. A dog that feels as if his space is invaded while eating will automatically go into "pack leader" mode because he is feeling that his food is threatened….And this is counterproductive to the goal.

From the perspective of a puppy, adult dog, or senior dog….If they feel as if there is too much noise or they fear that people are coming too close to their food, they will not be able to relax. Senses will be heightened and a dog's mind will revert into a state of "leader" which is the opposite of what you want to accomplish. With this being said, we can go on from here with the assumption that you have chosen a quiet eating area for your dog and that no one bothers him while he is eating.

The very first thing that must happen before a dog is given his food is that the dog must sit. And by "sit", this means a solid sit on the floor, holding still until released from the position. It does not count if a dog only sits because he feels like doing so. A dog must be encouraged to go over to the designated eating area and be given the command.

If your puppy or dog is not yet fully trained to sit on command, this training must happen first. We will go over how to successfully train a dog of any age to sit. If your dog already knows this command and follows it each and every time, feel free to skip over this section.

What You Should Know About This Command

Training a dog to sit is one of the easiest commands to teach, yet it is one of the most important ones. It is the basis for many other commands. It is used in a wide variety of situations. Teaching this command serves two purposes: It will be used for establishing leadership with proper feeding methods, and at the same time, just the process itself of successfully teaching the command will help to establish you as the Alpha.

The goal of this command is that when the command "Sit" is given, your dog will sit squarely and firmly down on his hindquarters and remain sitting until you give the "release" word.

Puppies as young as seven weeks old can start learning this command and it is often the first command that a dog is taught. Have two training sessions each day. It is best to have them be spaced apart, with perhaps one in the morning and one in the early evening. If morning is not a good time for you, you can practice once in the early evening and once a couple of hours later but not within an hour of "bedtime".

Treats play a huge role in enticing your puppy to follow this command. Therefore, your dog should be hungry when you do these training sessions. However, be sure that your dog is not starving for dinner as he will be too fixated on wanting to devour a full meal and not be able to stay focused. He should be hungry enough that the treats are desired.

The treat should be a special reward and not a snack that you would normally be giving to your dog anyway at some point in the day.

One food that works very well in this situation is crisp bacon. Bacon is actually not an unhealthy food if it is given in moderation and prepared properly. Pre-cooked bacon works well and you can microwave it to a very crisp texture. Doing so releases much of the fat. Then, you will want to put the pieces between paper towels and squeeze it all together, so that the paper towels soak up most of the remaining fat. What you are left with are crisp pieces that are 95% meat.

One piece of pre-cooked bacon that has been microwaved for 20 seconds and fat has been soaked up with a paper towel contains 15.5 calories. It contains 5 grams of protein. It contains 5 grams of fat (which is needed as part of any food plan, especially for puppies). It is best when cooked well, allowed to cool and then crumbled. When done this way, one piece can be used for two reward times. Each reward will contain only 7.75 calories.

While each puppy has his own learning rate, your puppy will be able to master this command in one to three weeks. End on a "high note" when your puppy is doing well even if you must go back to an earlier step in order for him to hear "Good Sit!" Give praise for "good attempts" and work to keep the morale high. Never say "No" and say "Uh-oh" instead so that your dog does not become discouraged by feeling "wrong".

 Choose a room that has little distractions. You may also wish to do this outside, but again it should be an area with few (or no) distractions.

Have a treat in your hand, and also some in your pocket.

 Have your dog on leash.

 Stand or kneel right in front of your dog, holding a treat in your hand a little higher than your dog's head.

 Slowly move the treat straight back over your dog's head. This should cause his nose to point up and his rump to drop down to the floor. If his rump does not drop, keep moving the treat straight backward toward his tail. The very moment that his rump touches the floor, give him the treat and signal the desired behavior by saying, "Good Sit!" in a happy voice.

Note: It is important to say "Good SIT" and not "Good Boy" or "Good Girl" because saying "Good *Sit!*" reinforces the command, allowing your dog to have a better understanding of *why* he is being rewarded.

Once your dog has shown you that he sits when commanded in this way, move on to the stage of waiting a few seconds before giving him the reward. Remember to only reward while your dog is in the correct position of squarely sitting on the floor.

 Slowly increase the amount of time that you wish for your dog to sit. Start with just a count of three seconds. When you are ready for him to come out of the "Sit", say "Okay" (the release word). Say it as if you are saying, "You are free!" and use a hand motion to send that message.

When your dog moves out of the sitting position, offer him praise and a pat. Do not offer a treat, but do make it clear that you are happy that he not only sat, but came out of the sit when you released him with the word of "Okay".

Possible Hiccups

If your dog jumps at your hand that is holding the treat:

If this happens, hold the treat lower.

If your dog sits, but then keeps getting up before you release him with the "Okay" release word:

In a gentle but firm way, keep placing your dog back into a sit. Be sure to not give the treat until he has been in the position for a count of three.

Back to Feeding Properly

If you needed to teach the "Sit" command to your puppy or dog and you have done so...Or if he already knew it well, it is now time to continue on with the feeding process instructions.

It is best to feed your dog at the same time that you and other family members are eating dinner as well. Due to busy schedules, this cannot always be done; however if you have the chance to eat a meal and have your dog eat at that time as well it will only be beneficial.

 The average dinner time for Americans increases each year. In 1990 it was 5:30 PM...Now it is 7:47 PM! For those polled, over 50% blamed their busy lifestyle as the reason for eating at this later time.

One of the tips to remember during this process is that your dog may show resistance to this new method. He may beg, whine, jump up and down and basically try his best to disturb you...All in an effort to immediately be given his meal. It is important that the meal be given to him when YOU decide to do so. He must not think that it is given because he barked and jumped around sufficiently to cause you to give it to him.

If you will be eating a meal at the same time that you feed your dog, you will want to prepare his food ahead of time and leave the bowl up on a kitchen counter. If you have a puppy this causes no problems. If you have older, larger dog do be sure to that he cannot reach the bowl by jumping or maneuvering up onto chairs to reach it. You will sit down and begin eating. Chances are that your dog is now going to act bananas. Ignore the behavior. When both you and your dog are eating within the same time frame, he must see and *clearly* understand that you are eating first.

The leader of the pack *always* eats first. This is a basic rule that goes back thousands of years, even before the domestication of dogs. It is a primal instinct. It is a rule understood by all canines that the one in charge demonstrates his rank in this way.

Many owners do not think about this and they normally have a routine of placing down the dog's bowl and then sitting down themselves to enjoy a meal. This sends out the wrong message and it does so in a *massive* way. Just this action alone can cause a dog to question their human's authority. This can single-handedly cause a puppy or dog to act out and feel as if he does not need to answer to anyone in regard to behavior.

Therefore, you will begin eating for at least a solid 30 seconds. Then, you will get up from the table to retrieve your dog's bowl. If you are *not* eating at the same time as your dog, you will begin at *this* point, of holding the bowl in one hand. Hold it high enough so that your dog can see it and smell it but not reach it even with the highest of jumps.

Now, it is time to command your dog to "Sit". Giving this command causes a dog to pause, stopping any negative behavior such as jumping up...Therefore, once obeyed, he will know that the food was given to him because you decided to do so, and not as a result of jumping, barking or trying to gain your attention.

As described earlier, the "Sit" must be solid and your dog must hold still in that position until you release him from it. If he breaks out of position, the bowl cannot be given to him.

It may take one try or twenty tries, however once he is sitting and waiting for what will come next, you can then release him by saying "Okay" and then place the bowl down. You have now just taught your dog a highly valuable lesson. It has been made very clear to him that receiving his food (what he considers to be his main need for survival) was a *marked, deliberate* decision made by you (or whichever human family member did so).

Treats

You may be giving your puppy treats as reward for training and that is just fine. When done in that way, he is learning that: Listening to your command = receiving food, and this helps to reinforce the fact that you are the leader.

If you give treats randomly, perhaps done between meals to simply offer something tasty, it must be done in a similar way that meals are given. The treat should only be given after a dog is commanded to "Sit" and stays in position until released with the word of "Okay".

For both meals and treats, your puppy or dog will be thrilled to be given something delicious and he will appreciate that you gave it to him. Never allow yourself to think that it is wrong to demand that a dog "Sit" for you in order to be given a snack or a meal.

While we like to think of our dogs as part of our family, and indeed they are, we cannot forget that they are canines. As canines, they will have certain behaviors such as chewing, tugging, nipping and biting…Your role as owner (and leader) is to make sure the household runs smoothly.

When a puppy or dog is chewing, tugging, nipping or biting this cannot equal a happy, peaceful household that is exists in harmony. Yes, your dog will be "under" you in regard to rank in the "pack"….He cannot be equal and he certainly cannot be your leader. In order to chaos to cease, he must be "under" you; and as stated earlier, you can be the most loving, caring leader in the world.

The Order of Arriving and Departing

Another element that will establish you as the leader, thus allowing you to be in control and to be *able* to stop chewing, tugging, nipping and biting issues will be how you enter and exit the home with your dog. Many owners do not think about this at all. When it is time to go out for a walk, an owner often prepares by gathering water that may be brought along, by connecting the leash, etc. However, they do not think about anything in particular when passing through the doorway. Have *you* ever given thought to this?

As we talked about earlier, dogs feel safe and secure when they are in an established pack. They feel relieved of the pressures of struggling with the question of who is the leader if it is not clear to them. Owners can sometimes give their dog the wrong impression without knowing it and an improper method of entering and exiting is a *major* one.

Just about as equal in impact as the feeding method that you have read about is the order in which you enter and exit your home. In a pack (your family), the leader always enters the den (your home) first and the leader always exits the den (your home) first. To allow your dog to exit first is the same as saying, "Yes, you go ahead first, I bow to you, you are the leader and therefore it is your rightful place to lead us out of the home".

This is not a message that you want to convey. An owner cannot expect a puppy or dog to not chew, tug, nip and/or bite when they have essentially told him that he is in charge and can do as he pleases. He will be very reluctant to listen to your commands to stop a behavior if you have placed into his mind that you are handing over the reins of leadership.

Some owners may think, "Well, my puppy just runs out the door as fast as he can, I can't control *that*!" With the proper length of leash and with a proper collar or harness, an owner can have *all* of the control.

For toy and small breed dogs - It is always suggested to use a harness as opposed to a collar for safety reasons. All small dogs under the weight of 20 pounds are susceptible to collapsed trachea. While this condition can develop for other reasons, collapsed trachea can occur if too much pressure is put on a dog's neck. The cartilage rings that surround the trachea can be crushed; the rings can break inward causing not only moderate to severe pain but it also can cause breathing and eating problems. It is a serious injury.

When on leash and *collar*, a puppy or dog can leap forward, off to the side or up…And if the leash goes taut, all pressure is put onto the dog's neck. When using a harness, pressure is distributed across the chest, shoulders and back. Therefore, not only does a harness greatly reduce the odds of your puppy or dog becoming injured while on leash, it also gives you much greater control while you are walking him. Consequently, owners of toy or small breed dogs should always be using a harness regardless.

For medium, large and giant breeds – While larger dogs are not as prone to collapsed trachea to the degree that smaller dogs are, using a harness provides an owner with much more control than a collar. Have you ever seen a person basically being dragged down a street by their dog while going for a "walk"? With proper training for "Heeling", no owner should ever be led by their dog; and using a harness will be a step toward gaining control.

For all puppies and dogs - Harnesses are now very popular and it is commonplace to use one. They can be found in a huge assortment of materials and methods of connection. A dog may show reluctance when it is slipped on, however he will soon become used to it. They are neither heavy nor uncomfortable; for a dog that is only used to a collar, it is simply new and after a few times of wearing one, the dog will adapt.

Back to the subject of having control when you enter and exit the home… Now you understand why you (and all other humans) must enter and exit first. You also now understand the importance of using a harness no matter what the age or size of your dog, as it will allow you to have control over the order in which you all enter and exit.

Perhaps you are using a retractable leash or perhaps you are using a standard 6 foot leash. Either way, when it is time to exit the home, it will be easiest to have control if you have the leash connected to the harness and then keep the leash at a length of 2 to 3 feet depending on the size of your puppy or dog.

Do not attempt to exit until you are completely ready. Therefore, have water, your keys and any other needed items already on you. Everyone should have shoes on, jackets on, etc. Once you (and any other people) are ready to leave, your dog should be given the "Sit" command. When he is holding the position, the leash should be connected to the harness. The dog should then be praised with "Good Sit", and released with "Okay".

Now it is time to leave. With the leash in one hand, extend that arm out to keep your dog inside of the home, yet very close to the door. All humans should exit at a normal pace. You (or the person holding the leash) will exit and then allow your dog to exit. This must be repeated any time you are *entering* the house.

The order in which people enter and exit is not of great importance; it can be mother, son, daughter, father and then dog....or son, daughter, aunt, family friend and then dog. However, everyone who lives in the home should take turns being the one who will hold the leash and be in control of your dog entering and exiting last.

It is highly suggested to include children in this process. As with the feeding element described earlier, children must be seen as leaders as well. You will want your children to be able to command your dog and have your dog listen to them. If your puppy or dog is tugging at, nipping and/or biting at your children you will certainly want them to be included in all of this training.

Even if your dog is only nipping at you and is not doing so to your children or anyone else in the home, this can change. Therefore, all humans should practice doing this and do so on a regular basis so that your dog never sees only one certain person as the leader.

The Ultimate Method

This next method, when used in conjunction with the other methods, sends a very clear and distinct message that you are the undeniable leader. Before doing this please be very aware of how fragile your puppy is. Even large and giant dog breeds are fragile during puppyhood (at least compared to how strong they will be when an adult).

Toy and small dog breeds are incredibly delicate. Their bones are tiny. As puppies they do not yet have a sufficient layer of muscle to protect the stomach against even moderate force.

When doing this technique of showing that you are leader, it must be done with the utmost care. You must deliberately be gentle and have complete control over the strength (or in this case non-strength) that you will be using. Since a puppy can be injured, sometimes quite severely, if this is done with force, do not allow any young children to participate in this method unless closely supervised.

Only if you understand the great importance of doing this with abundant care and with the mindset of doing it in a loving way….And only if confident that you will do so without causing harm should you continue. With the significance of doing this in a very loving and non-harming way firmly understood by you, one time per day you will want to sit beside your puppy on the floor. Place a soft, clean blanket on the floor beside you. A baby blanket works very well.

Gently place your puppy down, with his back on the blanket, and his front facing up toward you. You will then spread your hand and very gently place it over his stomach. Do not use force. You will only want to use *just* enough strength to be able to hold your puppy in place.

Do not have an overly serious look on your face….You can even speak to your puppy by saying something to the effect of "Okay there, silly, just hold still". Most puppies will begin to wiggle as they will not want to be submissive to you. They will try to evoke their *potential* of being leader and work their way out of the hold.

Be patient. With no other option, your puppy will stop wiggling. Once he stays stills this means "I yield to you, I agree that you are my leader".

Done consistently, this gentle way of showing your leadership will secure your role as Alpha and allow you to be able to have success with the upcoming training for chewing, tugging, nipping and/or biting.

Important Tips

The specific methods of feeding and of entering and exiting the home are the two most important elements of teaching your puppy or dog that you are someone who must, by resolute canine instinct, be listened to. If an owner only does one of them…Or only does these things randomly and not consistency each and every day, it will have little impact.

This works best with a puppy that can be taught this from an early age; but owners of older dogs should not despair. You most likely know that an old dog *can* be taught new tricks. For adopted older dogs or even for older adult dogs that simply did not learn these lessons during puppyhood, they can certainly learn them now.

The goal will be to establish yourself as leader and at the *same* time be teaching your dog to not chew, tug, nip or bite. However, there will be a window of time in which your leadership is not yet established. It can take anywhere from one week to one month for a dog to fully understand the rank of those in the home. During this time, stay firm in your trainings for both the leadership role talked about here and for the following specific training for chewing, tugging, nipping and biting.

While you are following the training for behavioral issues, your dog may not be *fully* listening to you at first. But, you must be resilient and continue on. As your dog gradually learns that you are the leader, *there will be a shift in how he responds to the training.*

Therefore, do both types of training at the same time.... You will want to begin working on teaching rank and then after a week or so, start in with the following behavioral training so that you will ultimately be teaching both simultaneously.

The methods of feeding and entering and exiting should be done for life. When you first begin this, the lessons will be teaching your dog that you (and any other humans in the home) are Alphas. It is important to continue on with those methods once rank is established. If not, a dog will revert back to trying to take on the leadership role.

For example, if you feel "safe" that your dog sees you as leader and you go back to allowing him to exit the home first, he will see this as a "weakness" and a "sign" from you that you have become unsure about your standing as Alpha.

Two things will then happen: Your dog will begin to feel stressed since his instinct will be telling him that leadership may be breaking down...This places him in an unstable environment in which he questions the strength of his "pack".

Secondly, in response to this turn of events, he will watch you carefully...If you were to continue to show this "weakness", he would step up and try to take control of the Alpha position. He won't even be doing this because he "wants to"...he will do this because canine instinct dictates that the "pack" simply "must" have an Alpha and since he sees you as "stepping down", he will take over the role in order to keep the "pack" functioning. He will then stop listening to commands, nip when irritated and essentially trot around as if he runs the home.

Making these methods "everyday" guidelines will ensure that your dog never forgets.

Other Things You Can Do To Establish Yourself as Leader

In addition to the feeding and entering and exiting methods, other elements can add to the fundamental fact that the dog does not rule the house. They are not very effective on their own, but when done in addition to the preceding they will contribute to the overall message that must be taught.

All elements of grooming (brushing, giving baths, trimming nails and all other care) sends a message as well. Whenever any grooming or care is done, the dog should be given the command of "Sit" and then only while politely and nicely in position should the brushing, trimming and other tasks be done.

On average, most dogs need:

- **Baths every 3 weeks**
- **Nail trims every 6 weeks**
- **Brushing varies...From every 3 days to once per week, depending on the breed of dog that you have.**

Be Sure of Things before Continuing On

If you believe that you have established yourself as the leader, do take a moment to think about your certainty of this. Perhaps your dog does sit before you offer a meal, but do you allow him to see that you are eating first? Perhaps you do allow him to see that you are eating first, but does every person in the home take turns with feeding? Do be sure that this is all set in place and then continue on.

Teething – Help Your Puppy Get Through this Difficult Time & Simultaneously Save Your Home

If your puppy is teething and you are dealing with chewing issues, it will be very helpful for you to read about this section before moving ahead.

At about the age of 4 to 6 months, puppies will begin to lose their "baby teeth" (deciduous teeth) and their permanent, adult canine teeth begin to grow in. Puppies almost always lose their teeth in a specific order:

First the smaller front teeth, then the premolars, molars and finally the canine teeth come out.

Often, the puppy's deciduous teeth will fall out while eating or playing, therefore they can be swallowed and you may not notice that it has happened. The teeth are so tiny that they are usually swallowed without causing any discomfort or health issues.

If at the age of 6 months, your puppy is still holding onto his puppy teeth, you should have a veterinarian perform a dental checkup. In rare cases, an adult tooth will come in slanted and may affect the other teeth.

The loss of puppy teeth and the growth of adult teeth normally happen in this order and time line:

- ✪ 4 Months old - the incisors begin to grow in

- ✪ 5 months old - the canine teeth begin to grow in

- ✪ 6 months old - the molars begin to grow in

By 8 months old, a puppy should have all teeth fully grown in and teething will stop. Do keep in mind that some puppies are late bloomers and teething may last a bit longer.

When an Adult Tooth Grows in Before a Puppy Tooth Falls Out

Sometimes, an adult tooth will begin to drop down while the puppy tooth is still in place. A puppy may then have double row of teeth. This can happen with one tooth or with several.

With the puppy tooth in the way, the adult tooth may grow in crooked. This can cause: Discomfort, cuts to the inside of the puppy's mouth and/or eating and chewing problems.

Therefore, if this situation happens, you will want the veterinarian to take a look at your puppy's teeth. Most likely, the puppy tooth can be pulled out without sedation. Doing so will allow  the adult tooth to grow in properly.

 Many people believe that "puppy teeth" do not have roots. This is actually not true. Each puppy tooth does have a root; it is very thin and very long. Each adult tooth will grow up from where the tip of the deciduous tooth's root is. That root is absorbed during the process. This is why it is important to have any puppy teeth removed by a veterinarian if they do not come out naturally...He will make sure that the root is removed as well, something that an owner simply cannot do.

Helping with Teething Discomfort

When a puppy is teething, he has a strong, uncontrollable urge to chew on anything and everything. This is one reason why an owner must puppy-proof the home, to keep any dangerous items away from the reach of the puppy, such as electrical cords. There is no excuse for an owner being dismayed that a puppy chewed on an electrical cord; the cord should never, ever be in reach.

Your puppy will not understand the difference between chewing on your favorite shoes and chewing on a teething toy. All that the puppy knows is that chewing makes him feel better and helps to relieve the discomfort that his teeth are causing. There are several things that you can do to get through this phase without your puppy chewing up the house and help your puppy at the same time.

Teething toys-   This is a must. A teething toy is much different than a basic dog toy. A teething toy is one which has *two* main elements:

 It is shaped with safe projections coming out of it. These smaller parts of the toy are so helpful for teething puppies. They will work these parts into the small areas of their gums to "hit just the right spot".

It is designed to be frozen. When a puppy is teething, having a cold toy to chew on offers a lot of relief. Many teething toys are made to hold water. When you freeze them, a puppy will chew on them for hours as the frozen ice gradually changes into a cool slush. After an hour or so, you can offer another frozen toy that is waiting in your freezer.

 If your puppy does not seem interested in his teething toys, it can be very helpful to spread a dab of plain peanut butter on one…This will initiate desire and once the puppy learns that the toy helps with his discomfort, he will be more prone to look to it for relief.

Ice cubes- This will not only entertain you, but will help make your puppy feel better. Most puppies find it amazingly fun to chase an ice cube around on a slippery floor, such as one made of linoleum or hardwood. The ice cube's cold temperature will offer relief to the puppy's gums.

A frozen wash cloth- Take a clean washcloth and soak it with clean water. Wring it out by hand, shaping it into a rope-like shape. Then, place it in the freezer until it is frozen solid. As a puppy chews on this, the cold will numb the teething pain.

Helpful Tips

Teething puppies are looking for one thing: Something to make the pain go away. They will chew on anything that is readily available. For this reason all shoes, pocket books, clothes, etc. should be put out of reach during this phase. If it is not within reach, your puppy can't chew on it. Teething toys (along with ice cubes and frozen washcloths) should be offered and available at all times. One "chew element" should be with the puppy and at least two in the freezer, ready to be switched out once the current toy loses its coldness.

If your puppy needs to be left home alone during the day for a moderate amount of time, you can do a couple of things to help:

 Obtain a small plastic cooler. Be sure that there are no small pieces that the puppy can chew off. Leave the cooler in the puppy's area with the lid completely off. Place 4 to 5 frozen teething toys inside. The insulation of the bottom and sides of the cooler, along with the coldness of the frozen toys will keep those toys cold for many hours.

 Be sure to confine your puppy to a gated off area or place the puppy inside a playpen; where the environment is safe and there is nothing dangerous that the puppy can chew on except for his teething toys.

Now that you know how to help your puppy with teething discomfort, it is time to now discuss how to teach him what is acceptable and what is not. Ahead in the next chapter we will discuss in detail the exact steps that you will want to take to stop any unwanted chewing behavior.

Chewing – Training to Limit Chewing to Toys and Food Only

A Puppy's Need for Discovery and Your Role to Set Limits

When a puppy or dog chews on any other objects other than his dog toys, this can be a huge problem. Puppies may chew on non-acceptable objects due to teething and then if the behavior is not stopped, they can continue on and be chewers for life. Even if a puppy is too young to be teething or if he is over that process by now, he may still chew. This is because mouthing objects is the main method of figuring out what something is. This is especially true for puppies, since so many things are new and the urge to explore is high. Each day is a discovery of new sounds, new smells, new sights and new objects.

A puppy and even older dogs can become quite used to the behavior of mouthing an object and chewing on it to figure out its qualities. "Does it have a taste?" "Does it have a texture that feels good to me?" "Does it make an interesting noise when I chew this?" These are all questions that are metaphorically running through a dog's mind when he is chewing on something. He is in the process of discovery.

If he finds that the answer is an advantageous one and if no one of authority (you) steps in to stop him, he may seek out and chew on a certain object at every single opportunity. This is why some owners talk about how their dog always chews on socks. This is because the dog found it to feel good and no one *of authority* stopped him from doing so to teach him that chewing on them is inappropriate.

When a puppy has a chewing problem and an owner is trying to help him resolve it, temptation must be removed. Think about a person who is trying to diet. In one scenario that person's refrigerator and cabinets are filled with potato chips, pizza, cheeseburgers, bacon, ice cream and cookies.

In another scenario that person's refrigerator and cabinets only contain fruits, vegetables, skinless chicken meat, egg whites and low fat milk. That person does not have the ability to leave the home to purchase or obtain any other food than what is there in the home. Which scenario presents the likelihood of having the most success in eating a healthy diet? Keeping this in mind, if the object is not there for a dog to chew it, it will not be chewed on. It sounds easy enough, but it cannot be done unless you take the time and put the effort into moving objects and finding new spots for them.

You do not need to rearrange your entire home. You must look at things from the perspective of your dog. What is within reach? What is small enough to be mouthed? What has the right texture that it may be tempting? You cannot remove your sofa and we will soon talk about the details of stopping your dog from chewing on things including furniture. However, you can remove 70 to 80% of the possible small objects that a dog may chew on that you do not want destroyed.

Shoes, clothes, remotes, keys, toss pillows, pocket books, wallets and other objects of this type can be kept up on shelves, in closets, on countertops, in baskets that are placed on tables or in other places that a dog simply cannot reach.

 Pet insurance claim adjusters list the 10 items most commonly swallowed by dogs that result in having them surgically removed as being:

Socks, underwear, panty hose, rocks, balls, corncobs, bones, hair ties, ribbons, and jewelry.

A puppy, an adult dog or a senior may chew due to boredom. With no one to play with and nothing interesting to do, a dog often will chew away on something...If only because it provides *some* sort of stimulation even if ever so small. If you feel that this may be the cause of chewing or one of the causes, it will be important to do two things: Move any objects that your dog can reach to a spot that he cannot reach and offer more stimulation.

When you are home try to include your dog in the things that you do. You can bring him outside while you garden or encourage him to sit beside you while you watch a movie. Be sure to take him for at least one walk per day to release pent up energy. Devote a half hour of your day for play time. Choose another half hour for command training.

When you are not home, do not leave a puppy in a crate for many hours. It will cause him to become overly stressed and then he will act out when he is released. Better is a playpen or gated off area. A radio should be playing in the background (out of reach). Toys that make noise and toys that hold treats inside should be available. A clean soft comfortable resting and sleeping area should be in the pen or gated off area.

If no humans will be home for longer than six hours, it is highly recommended to make arrangements for someone to come over and walk your dog…This helps with housebreaking issues and being able to walk around while having interaction with a human *greatly* decreases the chances of boredom setting in.

You do not need to hire a professional "dog walker" as this can be expensive. If you have a neighbor, a family member or a friend who is free during the day, you may just be surprised that they are seeking something to do and walking your dog for you may sound desirable to them. You may also wish to consider hiring a reliable teenager who may be very happy to receive a few dollars for twenty minutes of "work".

Your Step-by-Step Training for Chewing

The most important element is that action must be taken the very moment that you see that your puppy is chewing on something other than his dog toys. As mentioned earlier, you have already taken the time to carefully go over your entire home to move any objects that are in reach of your puppy. That alone takes away a huge percentage of possible "victims" of chewing.

What to Do

As soon as you see your puppy chewing on something that he should not be, make a loud noise. It should be done with the intention of causing him to pause, not to scare him. Clap your hands or call out his name  loud enough to get his attention.

By following the advice in the "First Things You Must Do" chapter you have already established (or you are working on establishing) that you are the leader. When the leader makes a noise, a dog is ruled by canine instinct to immediately direct his attention to that leader. If it is teething discomfort that is causing the urge to chew to be very strong, a puppy's attention may be brief, this should be expected and this is why the next action should be done immediately.

Hand a permitted chew toy to your dog. This will be done in exchange for the object that he was chewing on. As you offer him the toy, say the word "Toy", "Chew" or any other word that you have chosen for this training. The main idea is that you will be teaching him that this word is connected to the toy and the act of chewing.

When he mouths the chew toy, say 'Good, Toy!" or "Good, Chew!" and then offer additional praise. "Good, *Chew!*" (Or "Good" with the word of your choosing said afterward) reinforces the action that your dog is taking.

While this *is* an exchange, do keep in mind that it is *non-negotiable*. If need be, you will take the object from your dog. In the best case scenarios, during that moment that you clapped your hands or loudly called out your dog's name, he dropped the object.

If he is chewing on a portion of a large, fixed object such as a sofa, as soon as you have gotten his attention, position yourself four to five feet away and encourage him to come to you where you will then offer the chew toy (Remember that if he is not receptive to it, dab a bit of peanut butter on it). Follow with the aforementioned reinforcement and praise.

If your puppy is chewing on an object, does not drop it, and he runs from you, do not chase after him. He would see that as a game. If he is trained for commands, this is the time to use "Come".

If he has not yet mastered this command, the best thing to do is to encourage *him* to chase *you*. Once he "wins" the challenge of catching you, you will then take the object and offer him the chew toy while saying "Chew". When he begins chewing on the toy, mark the good behavior by saying "*Good* Chew!" and then offer additional praise of "Good Boy!" or "Good Girl!"

The main goal will not be to scold or punish your dog for chewing on the non-toy object. This serves no purpose at all. It is counterproductive and will actually send the complete opposite message and lesson that you intend.

If you were to scold your dog, this is how it would be perceived by him: He was chewing and enjoying himself. His human called out his name. He dropped the object *or* had it taken from him *or* if chewing on the sofa he stopped and walked over to his human. Now, he is being yelled at or talked to with very negative tones. The dog now thinks that dropping the object or the action of his mouth letting go of an object is what causing his human to be angry. You do not want to teach your dog that the action of the object leaving his mouth equals you being angry at him. You will want the opposite to be true.

The key to success is to show your dog that chewing on an approved dog toy brings about good things. Immediately giving him a fun chew toy at the moment that he stopped chewing on the un-approved object while offering happy, excited praise shows a dog that he receives immediate benefit when following your guidelines.

Be sure to have chew toys readily available. This will not work if you say, "Hold on a moment", run into another room, grab a toy, jog back to your dog and then finally give it to him. A dog's mind loses the ability to make mental connections a lot faster than a human's mind and the opportunity to teach the lesson will likely have passed by.

You will want to keep containers of toys in each room that your dog may be in. While some toys should of course be within his reach, these containers of extra toys should be out of reach. They should be strategically placed so that you can quickly and easily grab a toy while doing this training.

Remember that your dog is not just listening to the words that you say, he is picking up on your tone of voice. While you *may* be genuinely very happy, there will be times when you simply need to put your acting skills to use. You will want to act as if he just did the most wonderful thing in the world. The tone that you use is just as important, if not more important, than the actual words that you say.

For example, when a dog begins to chew on an approved toy, you technically *could* say, "I am planning on cooking although I am not in the mood and by the way I'm worried about next week's meeting." And *if* you said *that* in a very happy and excited tone, your dog would get the message that you are pleased that he is chewing on the toy.

Teaching your dog that *keeping up* with good behavior brings about *even more* benefits will be of great help. Once you have given him the chew toy, keep a close eye on him for one to two minutes. If your dog is still chewing on the toy, go over to him while talking in a happy tone of voice, say "Good, Chew!" and offer him a treat.

It must not be a "normal" treat that is given for snacks throughout the day regardless of behavior. It must have great meaning. If a dog is routinely given the same type of small biscuit regularly throughout the day as a supplement to meals, and it is then given to him as a reward, it will not actually be seen as a reward. To a dog, it will mean nothing more than "Oh, a morsel of food, thank you".

As mentioned earlier, most puppies and dogs simply love bacon and it works well for training purposes. Another healthy "special" reward is turkey meatballs. You may wish to choose a different treat and that is fine. The important element is that your dog simply loves the taste and it is not a treat that is normally given out. It is an *extra* delicious treat that is *only* given as a reward for good behavior.

To recap what your dog experienced when following this training: He was chewing on something. He stopped chewing on that object. He started chewing on a dog toy. You, his wonderful leader, became very happy when he began chewing on the dog toy. He continued chewing on the toy and then he was rewarded again, not just with praise but with a taste of something absolutely delightful.

In a scenario of a dog experiencing this enough, driven by pure canine instinct alone he will begin to choose the behavior that is most beneficial to him. Chewing on the sofa (or any other off-limit object) only produced a small bit of happiness as the chewing urge was quelled and the object felt good in his mouth. Chewing on the dog toy produced *very* favorable results. Once he has chosen the most beneficial action, if the training remains consistent, he will choose this more and more.

Doing this *one* time may not mean much more than temporary satisfaction. The lesson will not be instilled in the dog's mind. What works is to do it each time that you witness undesirable chewing behavior and not skip any times. If this is done one day but not the next, a dog will not have a secure feeling of knowing what is to happen. Being unsure, he will revert back to what he *does* know: that chewing on the sofa brought some pleasure.

When the above training is done every day, by everyone in the house who sees the inappropriate chewing… there will be a moment when the dog's mind makes a switch. He will reach a moment of knowing. When done enough, he will not have the feeling of being unsure (which leads him to revert back to old habits). As soon as your dog feels secure in the fact that chewing only on toys produces very good results, you will both have achieved success.

Additionally, treats will not need to be given forever. Treats only need to be given for a relatively short amount of time. Why? Because after this is done consistently, a dog will then chew on his toys based solely on automated behavior. Chewing only on *approved* toys will become the dog's habit…In fact, many owners find that their dog becomes *very* attached to his toys after this training.

It is important to follow each and every piece of advice. Leaving out just one element often leads to failure. For example, if you do not have toys readily available within reach this will not work. If you use "normal" treats instead of an extra-special treat, it will not work.

Staying Successful

Your commitment to following this training is what will change the behavior of your dog. A dog that chews is not "bad", he simply has not been taught that it is to his advantage to only chew on dog toys. As his loving owner you can now teach him this valuable lesson and have a well behaved dog.

Once you feel that your dog has changed his behavior and is no longer a "chewer", it is very important to routinely remind him of these lessons. You do not need to praise and reward him every time that he is being good and chewing on a dog toy. However, every now and then...perhaps once per day...at the least every other day, do take a moment to offer praise and/or a small treat to remind him that he is behaving well and that you, the leader, are happy.

Tugging – When Your Dog Attaches Himself to You

Understanding This Behavior

Tugging is the act of mouthing a piece of your clothing (pants, shoes, etc.) and pulling with a moderate amount of force. It is not done with any intention of aggression. It is not done to express intolerance or irritation. A dog will nip and/or bite for those reasons and that sort of behavior is discussed in the following chapters. Tugging is an action that a dog, usually a puppy, will do to gain attention.

Dogs are creatures that, much like people, desire human companionship. They do not like to be alone. While a puppy may retreat to take a nap, an adult dog may retreat to savor the sun on the front porch and guard the home and a senior may retreat to find a quiet place to rest when presented with too much noise…Dogs in general like to be part of the family.

They want to be part of anything that appears to even "perhaps" be interesting to them. They want to be included in conversations (never mind that they do not understand most of the words being spoken).

 When your dog is listening to a conversation that you are having with another person, he may understand more than you think. The average adult dog understands 165 words. When an owner works hard to train a dog to understand words, a canine is capable of understanding over 200!

They want to know that their human is fully aware that they exist. They want care, comfort, praise and treats to be just an instant away, even if they do not expect to receive any at  that very moment in time.

Tugging is often a temporary phase of a dog's life, most often done during puppyhood when he can still have some insecurities. As dogs grow older, they gain a stronger sense of belonging in the family. When this happens, a dog usually calms down and feeling secure, the tugging will stop. However, you can't walk around for the next few months with your puppy clung to the bottom of your pants, now can you? So, let's see what you can do to discourage this behavior and encourage more acceptable behavior.

Unlike training for *other* sorts of behavioral issues, ignoring this behavior will not be part of this training as it is rather impossible to ignore a puppy adhered to you. Even if you can tolerate that your puppy is tugging on you while you are trying to watch TV or tidy up the house, it can cause injury to your puppy if he is accidentally stepped on or tripped over....And allowing the tugging to go on only encourages the behavior.

When a puppy is not told by his leader that his behavior is not acceptable, there are no disadvantages to the behavior and no benefits to stopping the behavior, he will continue on until he tires out (which can take a long time). Therefore the key is to make all of these things happen.

As with any type of training, success is only found when an owner is consistent with the training methods. This means that you cannot teach your puppy to not tug when you are walking around the home, but you then allow it when you are sitting on the sofa.

For this to work, everyone in the home must be made aware of the changes that are to happen. If there are children in the home, it is suggested to have a family meeting. Everyone should be told that a new rule is going into effect. All members of the household should be on the same page that the tugging behavior of the puppy is going to be dealt with by every person using the same training method, at all times, with no exceptions.

This is important, because if one person does all of the training and another person allows the tugging, nothing will be accomplished. In fact, it can actually make things worse. A puppy can become confused, which causes stress. Stress with puppies can cause other bad behaviors and it can actually affect health as well. In regard to hypoglycemia (a rapid drop in blood sugar levels), stress is one of the triggers for this dangerous medical condition.

In addition, if one person allows the tugging and another person is the only one doing the training, the dog can start to view the "trainer" person as showing "weakness" in leadership capabilities. We talked in great detail about how a dog must view all human family members as "leaders". If one person is not doing this training and another person is, the "trainer" will be unsuccessful. That unsuccessful person may then be perceived by the dog to not be worthy of the "leader" rank. He may then look to the inactive person as the true "leader" and confusion and chaos sets in.

Lastly, when one negative behavior is allowed, others often follow. When a certain behavior is allowed, it is the same as teaching a dog to do it. Therefore, *allowing* tugging is essentially *teaching* your dog to tug. Once a dog has learned to tug to gain attention, he often progresses to other forms of attention-seeking behavior such as barking, begging and more.

One very important thing to keep in mind is that your puppy may be tugging at you and trying to gain your attention for a valid reason. He may be doing this to let you know that he needs to go to the bathroom. It would be wonderful if every puppy sat at the door and rang a bell when they needed to be brought out the designated bathroom area. However, each puppy will create his own signal and therefore some will tug.

For this reason, before training your dog to stop this behavior, have a look at things to see if *this* is the intention of the puppy. If your dog just went to the bathroom ten minutes earlier, you can feel confident that he does not need to go out again. However, if you take note of when this behavior occurs and realize that your dog tugs at you (or others) only when it has been a while since he was brought outside, taking him out may be the answer.

You do not want to get into the habit of taking him outside each time that he tugs on you, if going to the bathroom was not the single reason for the tugging. If so, your dog may learn that tugging equals having some fresh air and being able to run around on the grass for a while. Therefore, test things out for a few days. If it appears that your dog is tugging only at times in which there is a possibility that he needs to urinate or have a bowel movement, do bring him out and see if that was the reason.

If you take him out four or five times, in response to tugging and he did not go to the bathroom, you should then continue on with the training to stop this behavior.

If you find out that the tugging was indeed an indication for the need to go out, it is recommended to not discourage it. If it was an indicator and you take action right away to bring your dog outside, the tugging will only last a second or so. And you should consider yourself lucky that your dog is actually signaling you as opposed to having an accident in the home (which technically would not be an "accident" since after all, he did let you know that he needed to be brought out).

Very young puppies (under the age of 12 weeks) may tug for other vital needs. A very young puppy may not yet understand that his food and water is always in one designated area. Alternatively, a very young puppy may not know where he should go to comfortably take a nap, and young puppies require a lot of sleep (up to 18 hours per day). For these reasons, if your puppy is 12 weeks or younger and he tugs at you, do lead him to his food and water….and if that does not satisfy him, do lead him to his soft dog bed.

 Canines sleep from 12 to 18 hours per day. This includes both nighttime sleeping and naps.

If you see that one of these two elements met his needs, then this means that this is just a very temporary phase of a young puppy not yet feeling secure and training to stop this behavior should not be done. Very soon, your puppy will learn that his food and water is always in the same spot and he will know exactly where to go to take naps.

So, now we know why a dog tugs. We also know why this behavior should be dealt with, *if* it should be dealt with at all. We also understand the importance of being consistent and having everyone in the home onboard with what needs to be done.

Your Step-by-Step Training for Tugging

It is vital to understand that causing discomfort or any level of pain to a puppy is barbaric. It is animal abuse and any owner who neglects or abuses a puppy should not be allowed to have a dog. Keeping this in mind, the training for tugging involves a brief displeasing sensation that causes no harm.

In many canine behavioral cases, ignoring the negative behavior and only rewarding the good behavior is what will work. In the case of tugging, things are very different. It is impossible to get across the message of "ignoring" while the puppy is clung to your clothing or shoes.

Additionally, while you may *feel* as if you are ignoring your puppy, if your puppy is tugging on you and is not stopped, he will *not* perceive this as being ignored. He will think that the behavior is tolerated; and that is the same as teaching him that it is perfectly okay to do it.

Therefore, you will want to obtain a small container of human mouth spray to freshen the breath. It does not matter which brand that you use. Often breath sprays are of a minty flavor and that does seem to work best. *Do not use a cinnamon flavor as it can cause a sensation of heat which can be too intense for a puppy.*

You will want to discreetly keep this in your pocket. If there are others in the household, everyone should be equipped with their own breath spray for this training purpose. When this is implemented, a puppy will then learn that if he tugs at one person and it is not beneficial, if he trots off to another person and tugs at them, it will bring about the same result.

When the tugging begins, you will avoid ALL eye contact with your puppy. Having any eye contact means that you are giving attention to him; since that is his goal, he "wins" and training will not be successful. Therefore, *without* eye contact, quickly spritz the mouth spray in front of your puppy's nose.

Do not press the container right to your puppy's nose! Nor should you hold it a foot away. It may take a few times for you to see which distance gains the desired result. With most puppies, a distance of five to six inches is appropriate.

As you quickly spritz it, you will say, "No" one time and then ignore the puppy. The spritz will cause him to discontinue the tugging. It is essential that you and ALL members of the household do not talk to him afterward for two full minutes (which is a long time for a puppy that is trying to gain attention).

If you talk to him before that time is up, it will be misinterpreted. A puppy may think that you are giving praise for the actual spritzing and that will cause a lot of confusion. Alternatively, despite the spritzing, he may think that the tugging worked to gain your attention.

Everyone will be ignoring the puppy and if he is to go to another person to tug, that person will repeat the spritzing step. Remember, no eye contact, no saying his name…He must be "invisible" to you and anyone else involved.

Only after two minutes of a puppy *knowing* that he is being ignored and having those two minutes be a time of no tugging, it will *then* be time to move on to the next steps.

Note: If tugging continues, spritzing and ignoring must continue…Do not worry about constant spritzing…A puppy often stops at one…and rarely will a puppy go back for a second spritz. You (and anyone else involved) will need to outlast your puppy. It is not always easy to ignore a puppy…you may think that it is not going to work…however, he will have a moment of realizing that his "pack" is not tolerating his behavior and he will sulk off.

Therefore, once you reach that moment of his understanding and allow two minutes to pass, praise will then be given.

The tone of your voice means so much. Be sure to say "Good Boy!" or "Good Girl!" with a happy, enthusiastic tone. After you give this praise, offer a toy. If your puppy will not take the toy, smear a small dab of peanut butter on it, as this will make it much more enticing.

The final part of this training is just as important as any part of it. It is the same as the previously mentioned end part of training for chewing, so we will be repeating this very significant element:

Wait an additional one to two minutes. If your dog is *still* not tugging and is doing any acceptable behavior (even if he is simply sitting there looking at you) go over to him while talking in a happy tone of voice and offer him a treat.

Remember that it must not be a "normal" treat, as it must have great meaning and that if a dog is routinely given the same type of small treat regularly throughout the day in addition to meals, if it is then given to them as a reward, it will not actually be seen as a reward.

You will want to offer the aforementioned bacon, turkey meatballs or any other food that will be perceived as being very special.

When a dog experiences this enough (done without fail, as described and never skipping a time or a day), driven by pure canine instinct alone he will then begin to choose the behavior that is most beneficial to him. Tugging at you did not produce good results at all. He felt a fast spritz of a displeasing sensation. Then, he was ignored…Not just by you, but by his entire "pack".

However, when he was *no longer* tugging, it produced *very* positive results. After a brief "banishment from the pack" he was let back in! Then, he received praise. *On top of that*, he *continued* to not tug and he received a special treat! Life could not be better for him right now, and he will learn that it was all due to not tugging at you.

Refraining from tugging *one* time may not mean much more than the temporary satisfaction of praise and then a treat. The lesson will not be remembered.

When the training is done every day, by everyone in the house who is tugged at, true understanding is reached. A puppy will understand the consequences of a chosen action.

After training has been instilled, treats will no longer need to be given, as a dog will refrain from tugging due to automated behavior. It will become *instinctual* to *refrain* from doing this. By pure canine instinct alone, he will learn that tugging = a dissatisfied "pack" and that not tugging = life is good. Since you used a toy in this process, a puppy will usually go to find that toy instead of tugging.

This training will not work for long if a puppy is in a constant state of feeling lonely. Since puppies tug to receive attention (when it is not due to needing to go to the bathroom as previously mentioned), it will be important to never allow your puppy to feel so isolated that he is desperate for someone to notice him or play with him. Canines *crave* human companionship.

Do be sure to pay plenty of attention to your puppy or dog when he is not tugging. It is best to talk to your dog randomly throughout the day. He does not need to understand what you are saying, hearing your voice is soothing to him. It offers a feeling of safety and security. Even a Great Dane or an Akita that stands guard protecting a home is still in need of reassurance that his humans love him.

When passing by your dog, reach out your hand to offer a quick pat. If you are planning on being at the computer for an hour or so, offer your dog an ice cube so that he can have fun with it as it slides around on the floor as you type away. If you are busy doing a household chore, give both you and your dog a break every now and then to play fetch for a few minutes.

When a puppy or dog is taught that attention will be given to him consistently and indiscriminately throughout the day and not when it is demanded, that puppy or dog will calm down and not act frantic to receive it.

Nipping – How to "Nip it in the Bud"

Understanding this Behavior

Nipping and biting are two completely different things. Nipping is a quick snapping of the jaws in the direction of a person. There may be skin contact or there may not be contact. It will be a fast "peck". For a short amount of time (from one second to one minute) a puppy or dog that is *going* to nip may display irritation (shown by acting anxious or uncomfortable) and then quickly nip. He *may* also nip without any warning at all.

When a dog bites, *aggressively* and *violently* bites, this is usually done with solid intention *and* after warnings have been given such as growling and a lowering of the tail.

This section will discuss nipping. If you are having issues with actual serous biting, you will want to refer to the next chapter of: Biting.

It can be very frustrating indeed if you have a new puppy or a new dog and things are not going as you envisioned. If you are having problems with your dog nipping, it is common and natural to feel frustrated and even a bit sad.

After all, your plan was to have a wonderful canine family member. You expected to have a dog to take for walks and cuddle up with on the sofa. You planned on having a friendly, happy and content pet. Now, if your puppy or dog is nipping, you may be wondering what went wrong.

It is normal for a person to feel downcast that they do not know how to stop a dog from nipping. It is also normal to have thoughts about whether you have gotten a "bad" dog; perhaps one that is out of control and simply is not fit to be a friendly companion.

While it is true that some puppies and dogs have serious behavioral problems and ultimately will not be able to be kept as canine family members, *this is rare.* If this is the case, it most often happens when an older dog is adopted. That dog may have a *lifetime* of *very* negative experiences that have added up to such an *intense* level that the dog simply cannot cope and live with humans as part of a family.

Dogs such as this often perceive danger and threat where none actually exist. They have lived through so many bad experiences and have been treated so terribly that they react and act out in anticipation of something bad being done to them even if it is never to happen.

If you have a *puppy* that nips, do understand that this *is* common. While it is not fun and it is exasperating for you, it is a common puppy behavioral issue that *can* be reversed.

Puppy Play

The majority of the first two months of a puppy's life is one of limitation. His world is small. During the first six to seven weeks, most of a puppy's interaction is with littermates, dam and owner. His littermates are *always* there and are the most accessible "play things".

The owner *may* not play a large role. So much depends on what type of owner oversaw the breeding. A small home breeder may take the time to interact with a puppy and begin to offer socialization…however at this young age, a puppy is *not* fully aware of his surroundings. He only absorbs a limited amount of information at this phase. And therefore *even with* interaction with a breeder, a puppy will not have a complete and genuine behavioral response.

In other cases of a large breeding program, very little interaction with humans may occur and even if it does, the puppy does not take in the entire weight of any situation.

Consequently, with deep curiosity and a strong instinct to play, one of a puppy's first activities aside from nursing and then eating will be to wrestle with his littermates. This is normal canine behavior. A puppy's cognizance is limited, and as a result, canine instinct dictates. This instinct tells him to play with his siblings and this "play" is *on a very basic level.*

Before the age of two months old and while living with the litter, a puppy is wrestling around with brothers and sisters and a lot of nipping is occurring. When a puppy nips another and it is strong enough to cause pain to the other, the offending puppy hears a loud yelp (which is quite startling) and then he is ignored. He is temporarily banned from the "pack". The dam may even enter the picture, using her nose to push the offender away and then ignore him as well, while giving attention to the "victim".

The lessons learned during this time, unfortunately, can be lost. During the time of transition, when a puppy is being prepped to go to his new home, is transported there and is trying to become accustomed to his new world, those lessons can be forgotten.

When a puppy *cannot* recall this lesson, he will revert back to what he knew and that inborn urge to nip during play is *strong*. A puppy does not have the ability to differentiate between his littermates and his new human family when it comes to play. With his brothers and sisters no longer present and available to interact with, a puppy will then turn to his humans for entertainment.

A nipping puppy does not know that his behavior is undesirable. For him, teachings learned during the newborn weeks have not been retained. A puppy has no idea that an action will not be tolerated unless he learns otherwise. For example, a puppy will mouth the most unpleasant of elements all in an effort to discover if he finds it to be worthy of being a "good" food. If it tastes bad, he will then learn that it is something to be avoided.

Puppies are active and always "on the go", each day, a puppy takes lots of actions. Each time an action is done, there is an opportunity to teach a puppy that it is either an acceptable action or that it is not acceptable. He will learn what *he* deems to be beneficial or not…and it will be an owner's job to teach a puppy what *they* consider to be appropriate or not.

With nipping, a puppy should not be considered to be "bad" as he simply does not know any better. With this said, nipping must not be tolerated. If an owner allows a puppy to nip he may nip forever. He may begin to nip at other people…at visitors and guests to your home and/or people that you encounter when outside of the home.

When a dog is allowed to do something, it is the same as teaching him to do it. Allowing a negative behavior, gives a dog the "okay" signal. An owner cannot expect a puppy to spontaneously stop nipping or to ever learn on his own that it is wrong. Additionally, if proper training is not introduced, owners can inadvertently encourage nipping behavior.

A Mean Puppy?

There are *other* puppies that will nip as a method of saying, *"Leave me alone!"* and this can be shocking and heartbreaking to an owner. "All I wanted was a cute, little puppy!" these owners will lament. If a puppy nips and it is clearly *not* intended as part of "play", this is undoubtedly a case of a puppy *not* perceiving their owner as the leader.

A puppy that thinks that *he* is the leader of the home can become *very* arrogant. Seeing an owner as his equal or *even* below him, a dog will then decide when he wants to be picked up, when he wants attention, when he wants to be petted…And if an owner does any of these things when the dog does not wish for it, that dog may nip.

He will nip because he sees no harm in doing so. Opposite to this, a dog will *not* nip or show any disrespect for his *leader*….However if the owner has not *unmistakably* established this relationship, the dog's personality can form into one in which he rules the home and controls the actions of the humans by nipping.

In this case, do please refer back to the chapter of: "The First Things You Must Do"…As it will be *very* important to first establish the proper relationship between you and your dog…and then proceed with training.

Before You Begin Training

So now we know the difference between nipping and biting. We know why a puppy nips. We also know why training must be done to stop the behavior. Finally, we know that *no matter what* the reason for a puppy nipping, before *any* training takes place (for any issue) that an owner *must first* take the steps to establish themselves as the leader, as the first chapter describes in detail.

Every person who lives in the home should understand the training that will take place and when it will begin. Part of the training for nipping behavior is to *completely and utterly* ignore the puppy; and if anyone strays from this a bit, all will be in vain. If this is done by three members of the household, but not the fourth, the training will not work. If this is done one day but not the next, it will not work.

As discussed earlier, ignoring is a *huge* statement. Once you establish yourself as Alpha and your puppy *knows* that he is under you (a Beta) in the ranking of his "pack" (your family), a brief period of ignoring will equal temporary banishment. For a puppy, this is unacceptable…Canines simply "must" live in a strong, well-run, solid, caring "pack".

When temporarily banished, a puppy will make fast adjustments to keep his pack running well. If *anyone* breaks from this training, it will put doubt in a puppy's mind. He will metaphorically think, "Well, *perhaps* the pack is not happy with me….A couple of my pack members *seem* to be alright with my behavior… Only one is *trying* to say that I should stop *but* I'm getting this message some days and not others… Hmmm, this message is *not* strong enough, it is confusing…It will be easier for me to continue on with nipping".

Training must be done no matter if skin contact is made or not. An owner should not make decisions on a case-by-case basis. For example, a puppy that normally nips the skin may nip in the air *near* a person; it should not then be overlooked because an owner thinks that the puppy is "behaving better than before". Any and all nipping behavior, including nips into the air that is directed at a person, must be dealt with in the same way.

Your Step-by-Step Training for Nipping

As soon as a puppy nips, action must be taken. There should be zero hesitation, aside from a second of shock that would be involuntary.

As we discussed earlier, the lesson that the puppy learned during the newborn weeks began by the "victim" of the nipping letting out a loud yelp. This is the basic and customary way that canines communicate to each other to relay that one is being injured or put into discomfort by the offender.

Since we cannot successfully get our message across by using our full vocabulary to our puppies, the best method for communicating with canines is to use a language that they *do* understand. Puppies and all dogs for that matter, usually only take in the first syllable of a word or the strongest sounding syllable, this is why commands are so short. Therefore, the very first thing that a person must do is to loudly and firmly say, "NO!"

Your "NO!" will be interpreted as a deep pitched, loud "yelp" that sends out the signal that the action was offensive. Unlike a littermate that did this in a high pitched tone (they were your puppy's equal in rank), it should be done in a deep tone of voice (since you have been working on establishing yourself as your puppy's loving and confident leader in the rank of the pack, as we discussed in the first chapter).

Now, there is a difference between loudly and firmly saying a word and yelling a word. Do not yell the word. You do not want to be yelling at your puppy all day. Your neighbors also do not want you to be yelling at your puppy. The idea is to startle your puppy with a clear signal that his action was offensive and that it will not be tolerated.

If you yell, it will take things to a higher level and can actually frighten a puppy, which can be considered to be animal abuse and/or neglect. A puppy that is routinely scared will grow up to have a host of behavioral problems and will never feel safe and secure. It is a form of emotional abuse and should not be done.

Also, it will not be helpful to say anything other than "NO!" Saying a full and complete sentence will not be helpful; and it will only delay you in taking the next necessary step.

If you are holding your puppy at the time of the nip, place him down on the floor. If you are outside and holding your puppy and he is not on leash, immediately go inside the home and place him on the floor. If you are outside and away from home, you hopefully have your puppy on leash; if so and if you were holding your puppy immediately place him on the ground.

If you were lying down next to your puppy, immediately stand up. If you were sitting down with your puppy on the floor, immediately stand up. If you were holding your puppy while sitting on a chair or sofa, immediately place him on the floor and stand up from the sofa or chair.

The idea is to not only place distance between you and your puppy but also to firmly establish yourself in a *physically* higher position to pronounce your rank as leader.

The next step to take, after you have assumed a leadership position by way of your body stance, is to 100% utterly and completely ignore your puppy. You may think, "Is he noticing that he is being ignored? He is just going over to his chew toy!"

While your puppy *may* indeed saunter over to his toys or walk over to the kitchen to lap up some water, the key to this is to maintain a strong and solid stance of ignoring your puppy up to and *past the time* that he will notice that he is being ignored.

Ignoring does not just mean not paying much attention to your puppy. Remember that this type of ignoring is akin to temporary banishment from the "pack". There must be *zero* eye contact. There must be *zero* verbal communication. There must be a *complete disregard* of any attention seeking behavior.

If there are other people in the home at this time, take care when speaking with each other, as you do not want your puppy to mistakenly perceive that he is being spoken to. At some point, typically within one to five minutes there will be a change. For very independent puppies, this can take up to fifteen minutes. However, remain firm and you will see that your puppy is going to notice that he is receiving zero attention. His leaders are not even making eye contact with him, let alone looking at him at all.

There is no petting, no one is holding him, and no one is offering toys, treats or even words. There will be a moment of clarification in which the puppy realizes that the "pack" (his humans) have banished him. Now his is metaphorically wondering, "Am I banished forever?" Worry sets in. The puppy is intelligent enough to know that his recent action caused this banishment.

Now, it is time to wait. Only when you see that your puppy is disturbed by this time of being ignored will you be close to the time of ending it. He may pace around. He may paw at you to gain your attention. He may bark, *but now is not the time to implement any barking training.*

You will know that a puppy has completely realized what has happened when he sulks away. Do not feel bad. You are teaching him a very important lesson that will allow him to be a happy, content and well-mannered dog.

Be sure that everyone continues to go about their business while utterly ignoring the puppy for five minutes *after* the time that he has shown signs that he is well aware of what has happened.

After those five minutes, do not go over and offer praise. For the strong negative behavior of nipping, reversing the banishment must be *earned*. This is the canine way. You can now look at your puppy. If he nudges you, you can respond with a light touch back but do not engage in any play or active interaction just yet.

After another five minutes, if the puppy has not nipped again, you may then allow things to go back to normal. Moderate play can resume. You can speak to him. No praise should be given yet.

After *another* five minutes, if your puppy has *still* not nipped again, it is time to go back to whatever physical positioning you were both in when that first initial nip occurred. For example, if you were sitting down on your favorite chair with your puppy in your lap, gently pick him up and place him on your lap. This creates a situation where the puppy must prove himself to the leader (you) that he has learned his lesson.

If your puppy remains behaving nicely and does not nip at you when in the same position as the nipping first occurred, it is *now* time for praise. Praise should be given in a happy tone of voice, with several "Good Boys" or "Good Girls" mixed in.

If you will remember from previous chapters, reward in the form of a treat was implemented to help with certain behavioral training. Nipping is a more serious issue than chewing, etc. since it is a physical offense directly against you or other family members.

For this reason, just being allowed back into the pack is reward. Your praise is additional to that. It took time to slowly allow your puppy back into the pack….Then you needed to test him by being in the same physical positioning as the initial nipping….And then time passed by when you confirmed that he was behaving.

Additional time was added on while you appropriately gave praise. Therefore, to offer a treat at this point would not be beneficial. Your puppy would not make the connection that it is associated to "not nipping". Since you cannot give a puppy treats all day long, it is best to save those treats for when they are needed (other types of training).

If at *any* time during any of these time phases a puppy nips again, *begin from step one* and continue on from there.

Tips for Success

 While you are in the process of training your puppy to not nip, do not engage in any play that could be perceived as encouraging nipping behavior. Many owners do this unknowingly. Most typical is a game of "tug-of-war", this should not be played as it only inspires aggressive behavior.

 The most common reason for a puppy nipping is that the puppy does not see their human as the leader. Therefore, be sure to carefully read Chapter Two so that you can begin teaching that very important element to your puppy.

 Remember that every person in the home must understand and follow the training technique.

 All training must be done each and every time that the puppy nips; there should never be a time when a nip is overlooked. One must never be too busy to correct this unacceptable behavior.

Do not give up; it takes more than one time for this to work. It will be the consistency of doing this each time that will lead you to success and having a puppy that is happy and friendly toward you and everyone else in the home.

Each puppy is different; some may learn to stop this behavior within a week, others may learn it after three weeks. Just remember that if this training is not done, those three weeks could turn into three *years* of nipping.

Biting – Behavioral Aggression that Must be Stopped with Proper Training

Understanding this Behavior

Biting is different from nipping. Nipping is a fast snapping of the jaws to show intolerance of a person or a situation. It can also be done as part of instinctual play. *Biting* is a *severe* form of aggression. When a dog bites, it is an intentional, *violent* act that sends a strong message.

With a nip being a quick snapping of the jaws often done in the air next to a person, biting is a *clenching* of the jaws into the flesh of a person. The jaws lock down, teeth sink down puncturing the skin and the dog may either stay latched on or retreat a bit but stay on guard.

The dog may send out warning before biting. However some may bite with no warning at all. Common warning signs are growling, showing of the teeth, a deep exhalation of air through the nostrils, pacing and/or staring at a person.

Do please make sure to read the previous Nipping chapter, as it is most likely the behavior that your puppy or dog is displaying, even though you or other people may *refer* to it as "biting". It is *rare* for a

household pet that is treated well and loved to turn on his humans and *aggressively* bite.

Training for this is intense and is very different than the needed training for nipping. Therefore, it is highly suggested to read through the entire previous Nipping chapter before deciding that your puppy or dog is actually a rare "biter".

First Check For This

First making sure that your dog does not have any injuries or medical conditions is very important. When a dog indeed bites (and not just nips) it is most often done out of instinct in reaction to pain. When a dog is in pain he often feels that he is in danger. Canine instinct is in control, telling the dog that since he is in pain (from illness or from injury) he is vulnerable due to being in a weakened condition. Even the most affectionate dogs will take a defensive stance during this time. It is quite common for a dog that is in pain to bite a human whom they love every much.

For this reason, if an otherwise normally friendly and loving dog has begun to bite this means that any and all possible health issues should be ruled out by a reputable and experienced veterinarian. There are so many injuries that a dog can receive without an owner ever realizing it until much later.

Luxating patella is just one. This is a genetic condition and can come on suddenly when the dog moves a particular way, jumps down from a certain height or while running. With this issue, the kneecap slips out of place. In numerous cases it is *initially* painful only for the split second that it is slipping. An owner can easy miss this.

Many times a dog will then show no signs of pain. As hours, days and sometimes even weeks go by, inflammation will set in. It is at this time that the dog will be in near constant pain. An owner can be puzzled regarding the dog's behavior as they "know" that the dog is not sick nor was he injured.

Therefore, always bring your dog for a full and complete checkup if he has suddenly started biting. Do this even if he just had a checkup a week ago. You never know what may have happened during that time. Injury can happen or illness can develop and cause pain within just a matter of hours.

If you are assured that your dog is in perfect health and you are completely confident that your dog is technically biting and not nipping, you can now start training your dog to stop this aggressive behavior.

This training (or any other training) will not work unless you are *unequivocally* seen as Alpha. Therefore, before you begin, do take a step back and read over Chapter Two, which discusses the very important aspect of establishing that you and all other people in the home are the leaders.

Different Channels of Severe Aggression

Aggression issues are usually seen channeled toward one of two separate elements, although a dog can display aggressive toward both.

There is aggression towards people. This can be strangers walking by or this can even be towards human family members. Some dogs simply will not tolerate certain people.   An example is the Akita. The Akita (both American and Japanese type) will rarely tolerate children, particular those who are not part of the family and are, to the dog, considered to be "outsiders". While there are exceptions, the owner of an Akita should be well aware that if the dog is not very well supervised when near children whom the dog is not extremely accustomed to, the dog may be very aggressive. And this includes biting.

There is aggression toward other animals. This problem will seem most severe if a dog is aggressive toward other dogs in the home or household pets. Some dog breeds simply do not tolerate smaller creatures. An example is the Beagle. He is a hunter at heart and while there are exceptions, most Beagles will not tolerate smaller animals. This includes rabbits, ferrets and hamsters. The Beagle will not just bite them; he will chase them down and be proud to bring you his captured "prey".

It is hoped that any owner of a dog has a clear understanding of that particular breed's ability to tolerate other dogs, animals and people. Training for aggression will not work at all if an owner tries to change the core instinct and temperament of a particular dog breed that has been bred over thousands of years to hold those traits.

The issue of mixed dogs comes into play while we are speaking of inherited traits of aggression. An Akita mix will often display the same aggressive tendencies as a purebred. A dog that carries Beagle genes may display the same hunter instinct as his purebred parent or grandparent. For this reason, if you have a mixed dog and know of the dog's ancestry, you should be aware of the characteristics of each of the breeds in his genetic makeup.

Of course, if you have a mixed dog and do not know of his ancestry, there is no way to know what aggressive traits he may have inherited unless you were to have DNA testing done to determine his genetic makeup. While this is available to pet owners, it is relatively costly and it will be a personal decision as to whether to have this done or not.

According to the Centers for Disease Control and Prevention (CDC), in regard to canine aggression that leads to a fatal attack, the top 10 most aggressive breeds are the Pit Bull, Rottweiler, Siberian Husky, Saint Bernard, German Shepherd, Great Dane, Doberman Pinscher, Chow Chow, Alaskan Malamute and Akita.

A study done by the University of Pennsylvania regarding aggression (but *not* actual attacks resulting in fatalities) shows a whole different picture. They found that some of the most aggressive breeds were toy or small breed dogs. Top on the list is the Dachshund, the Chihuahua and Jack Russell Terrier. Rottweilers, Chow-Chows, the Australian Cattle Dog, the Akita and Pit Bull are also included.

Even more surprising, a study in the UK revealed that one in five Dachshunds has bitten or tried to bite strangers, and 1 in 12 has shown aggression toward its owners.

Aggression Toward Another Canine Pet

If your dog shows aggression toward a new dog that has been introduced to the family this is often due to both dogs vying for the position of Alpha. As talked about earlier, your dog that lives in your "pack" (your family) must see *you* as the Alpha (leader). However, in *multi-pet* households, the animals will want to know "Who is the Alpha of the *animals?*"

Your dog will be working to figure out how this new dog affects the household and during this time, aggression can begin to show. Your dog will metaphorically begin to think "Is this other dog going to try to be in charge?" "Should I be the rightful Alpha Dog?" "Do I need to fight to take my place?"

Additionally, for your dog to get along with another dog, clear boundaries must be drawn and both dogs must be trained to understand how you expect them to behave.

Boundaries

Make sure that each dog has his own separate area. While it is nice to think that it would be cute for both dogs to be eating side by side or sleeping right next to each other, unless two dogs decide that they are comfortable with that, they must have their own spaces.

Be sure to give both dogs their own designated eating areas. The bowls should not be side-by-side. Envision that each dog needs an "invisible bubble" around him. It is best to have each dog eat in opposite corners of the kitchen.

If the food and water is placed too close together, the dogs will have a tendency to fight for what they consider to be their territory. If you see any aggressive behavior during feeding time, this means that you should place the bowls further apart.

Each dog should have his own dog bed or resting area. This is especially important if you have an older dog and a younger dog in the house together. Your older dog will want his own private area to retreat to when the younger dog is wearing him out. This can be in the same room, but in separate corners of that room. When you have dogs with a big age difference, it may be best to choose separate rooms.

Each dog should also have his own set of dog toys. It is best if these are kept in separate baskets in separate areas. The dogs may fight to claim a certain dog toy; however this will be discussed ahead.

This does not mean that your dogs will not interact or play with each other. This simply allows each of them to feel secure that what is most important to them will not be encroached upon.

Who is in Charge?

When you have two dogs, there will be a process of the dogs trying to figure out who is in charge in the animal subset of the "pack". Most of the time, the dogs will be able to decide this among themselves. And most of the time, it is the older dog who will be the Alpha. The other will be referred to as the Beta.

The Beta receives the same amount of love and attention from you…It is not necessary to feel "bad" for the Beta. Dogs are *very* uncomfortable when they do not feel secure in knowing the ranking of the "pack". There *cannot* be two Alpha dogs; without the matter settled, they would forever be vying for that *one* spot; there would be constant, never-ending tension and fighting. Therefore, one dog *must* be Beta. The dog that is Beta will feel at peace…loved, cared for and knowing that he belongs to a wonderful "pack".

When dogs decide this for themselves, there will be no actual aggression; however there may be some behavior that *may* be *mistaken* as aggression.

It is completely natural for an older dog to discipline a younger dog. It is *not* acceptable if strong aggression is shown and the younger dog is injured. However, for the home to run smoothly, you should allow the older dog to "put the younger dog in his place" *as long as there is no violence.* For example, an older dog may push the younger dog away if he gets too close to his toys.

As mentioned, *most of the time* it is the dog oldest in age that will take the role of Alpha…However, this is not always the case. A strong female may take the role and other times, the dog that lived in the home the longest *or* is the larger of the two will vie for the Alpha position. You will want to observe their behavior to see which dog desires to be Alpha more than the other.

Once you notice which dog is trying the hardest to become the "Alpha Dog", you can help both dogs get along better. How? The one trying hardest will show more dominance…he will reach his food first, he will be more "pushy". If the dogs have not quite fully set into stone which is the Alpha of the animals, there will be a time of turbulence. The pressure of a dog trying to constantly claim his role as leader is hard work.

You can help by giving the leading dog his food first. Following the proper feeding methods of establishing yourself as ultimate Alpha (you begin eating, the dogs are commanded to sit, only then do you place down food), you will want to place the Alpha Dog's food down first, wait 10 seconds and then place down the

Beta's food. When you are giving out treats, give a treat to the "Alpha Dog" first.

When you leave and then re-enter the home, *you* will exit and enter first (as described earlier), however the Alpha dog will be next, followed by the Beta dog. The Alpha should be "first" for all elements and then the Beta. When they see that you are agreeing with the ranking, both will come to an understanding quickly and aggression should cease.

Once it is established which dog is in charge, this does not give that dog a right to fight with or act aggressively with your other dog. Normally adjusted dogs are very happy with two dogs in the home or ten dogs in the home. If your dog growls at or bites your other dog this must be acted upon immediately.

Social isolation works best. A strong and firm "No!" followed by isolating the offending dog for at least 10 minutes is suggested. He should be placed behind a gate or other area where he will be able to see that he is missing out on being part of the "pack" (family) and only after obeying your "Sit" command and then released with "Okay", should he be allowed back into the group.

The more you work at helping your dogs establish who the Alpha dog is, and your actions confirm that, your dogs will stop acting hostile toward each other.

Finally, you may wish to think about having both pets spayed and/or neutered, as this greatly cuts down on territorial behavioral issues.

Training for Aggression Toward People

This can be a very frustrating situation; however training can help in many cases. Why would a dog show aggressive behavior toward people? There are several reasons, including:

Fear - Your dog may be afraid of strangers and the unknown. It can outwardly show by growling and even trying to bite people.

Improper Status - When a dog is aggressive towards human family members, this is often a sign that the dog is confused about his place in the family. Please refer back to Chapter Two if you have any doubts about this at all.

Health Issues – As we discussed, when any dog that is normally well behaved suddenly becomes aggressive, this very often is because the dog is suffering from some type of health issue.

Training for Aggression Toward Visitors or Strangers – ONLY if Biting Has NOT Yet Occurred

If your dog is only at the stage of showing aggressive tendencies *but has not yet bitten someone*, you may find success in training him to have control.

When this is a matter of a lack of socialization, your dog needs to learn that as long as he is with you, strangers are a normal part of life and he must behave around them. Particularly for breeds considered to have strong guarding abilities, it is not uncommon for a dog to be aggressive toward true strangers, who are coming to your home uninvited and unwanted.

Having your dog bark and show *some* aggression toward these types of strangers is not *necessarily* a bad thing as long as he does not bite. In the case of a break in, your dog's barking may just scare off the intruder. As long as your dog calms down once that person has left the property, all should be fine. *If* you approve of your dog protecting your home in his role as a "watch dog" you can say "Good Dog", give a pat and then show your dog that all is well by having calm actions and a matter-of-fact tone to your voice.

However, when you are walking your dog, if you are both in a social situation, or if you have a visitor to your home, you will want your dog to behave. This must begin by slowly teaching your dog what is expected of him and what is not acceptable. You will be training your dog to maintain control.

While there are always exceptions, generally speaking there are warning signs that are given before a dog bites. One must only understand what they are. The key is to step in and assert your leadership at the first indication that a dog is thinking about biting.

When a visitor comes over, have your dog on leash and harness (a harness is highly recommended since you will be able to quickly and safely reel him in, should make a motion toward your guest). While holding onto the end of the leash, give the command to "Sit", followed by "Stay". Only release him with an "Okay" when he appears to be calm. Remain holding onto your end of the leash.

After this point, the tone of your voice means a lot. Your dog may seem calm, but he is quite aware of the presence of another person and will be listening carefully to the conversation. All parties should speak in a happy, easy going, calm manner. This sets the tone that as the leader you do not see anyone as a potential danger.

When a visitor comes over, do not isolate your dog. This should never be the rule of what happens when guests come to the home. It sets a terrible guideline and does not allow a dog the opportunity to learn self-control and proper behavior. Only by being in the situation and receiving proper socialization training will a dog find and maintain control. While you are chatting with your friend(s) take note if your dog shows any signs of possible aggression/ biting.

Signs are: Sitting between you and them, standing between you and them, looking quickly back and forth between you and them, forcefully breathing out of his nose (almost a grunting noise), pacing, a direct stare (often accompanied with a lowered tail) and/ or growling.

If any of the above happens, immediately command him back into a "Sit", followed by a "Stay" in a spot close by but not in the middle of you and your company. If he gets out of the sit, instantly command him back into it. *This should be done in a firm voice, but certainly not in a fearful or apprehensive one.* You do not want to send a message that you are worried that without his obedience, he would immediately attack.

One must be poised, assured and assertive. An owner must show that *he* is in control and is leader of the pack. Alphas are confident in their status...therefore your goal is to speak as if you "know" that your dog will obey you. If you do not convey this, a dog will see this as "weakness" and will not be inclined to obey your commands or follow your lead. Praise will mean nothing and rewards will have little meaning.

Once your dog is sitting, continue to go about your business. Speak in normal tones. After a few minutes, if your dog is calm without showing any of the previously mentioned warning signs, you should then give him a small treat, let the leash out to give him more freedom of movement and go back to your visit.

It is important to NOT say anything to soothe him. This includes "It's alright", "It's okay", "Take it easy, everything's alright". This is because without the ability to understand all of your actual words, a dog understands the tone...and this is interpreted as praise. Additionally, never give a treat until he is calm.

Keep the first visit short, no more than fifteen minutes, knowing that the next visit will be able to be longer. For the *next* visit with the *same* visitor, repeat all steps...The difference will be that you will allow your dog to reach the point of receiving reward and then be free to do as he wishes, off leash, as long as he is not showing warning signs. Each visitor should have the first initial fifteen minute visit and then subsequent longer visits in which you release your dog if he is not showing aggressive behavior.

As you go through this training, you will reach a point of seeing a noticeable change in personality and behavior. When a dog fully understands that a visitor is not a threat, he will learn to relax.

Once composed and no longer on guard, he can become *very* bored. A dog that is prone to aggression needs to learn that *after* he has proven himself to maintain control, he will not be forced to endure what he may perceive to be a very uninteresting situation.

For dogs that showed aggression due to a lack of socialization, once that dog has "met" someone 5-6 times and all has been fine each time, you can now have that same person offer a treat if the behavior is as you expect. Once you reach this point, if it is someone that you see on a regular basis, there should be no problems, but always keep your eyes out for signs that your dog may be having trouble handing a situation. He may always be quietly listening and observing, but most often will not take action unless hectic behavior (yelling, throwing objects etc.) was to ensue.

Training for Aggression Toward Human Family Members

For aggression against family members (those whom a dog sees as members of his "pack"), social isolation training has been proven to work in many of these cases, *but not all cases*. If a dog's *core temperament* is a vicious one, this is *not* for an owner to try and change. *If* aggressive behavior is due to a dog taking the role of Alpha, this training often works.

This training is for dogs that show the aggressive warning signs of a ***possible*** bite. Remember that *nipping* is a quick snapping of the jaws but *biting* is when a dog's teeth sink in; there will be a severe *tearing* of the flesh...*it is a violent, hostile act.* Once again, this training that follows will be for owners who feel that their dog **may** *bite*.

If it is to work, it only works if it is followed precisely.

It will *only* work if the dog is aggressive due to not having a clear understanding that he is not the leader. Even if you have followed all of the previous training for establishing all humans as Alphas, in rare cases, a dog simply does not learn this important fact. Before beginning, hold a family meeting. Explain to everyone that *intense* training will begin and that it will require the help of everyone in the house. Four days will be dedicated to helping your aggressive dog with all of the pressure to be "leader" have the opportunity to change into a peaceful and calm family pet.

For this to work all family members should make every effort to have four uninterrupted days that they can stay home as much as possible. If this training does work, your dog will revert back into a loving canine family member and the four days will be worth it all.

Day 1 and 2- Full and Absolute Social Isolation

The dog must be *completely and utterly* ignored *except* for placing food on the floor for him (by following the method in Chapter Two in regard to the feeding method) and allowing him to go to the bathroom…(Do be sure to leave fresh water out at all times). Therefore, this means **zero** talking to him, **never** saying his name, **not** acknowledging him at all.

This also means giving **zero** interest to negative behavior. If the dog barks, no one must say "no". The dog must be ignored to *such* an intense level that he is essentially invisible. When we love our dog, this is very hard to do. It is difficult to ignore *any* entity that is in your close proximity.

However, one must remember that this is in the best interest of all involved. Only if you can train your dog to maintain control at all times will you be able to truly enjoy the benefits of ownership.

If your dog pushes against someone for attention, they must act as if the dog does not exist and so forth. It is essential that your dog *sees* all regular family members *and* is *in* the home with everyone...but is being completely ignored.

A sign that this training is working, is if your dog sleeps more than ordinary on Day Two. When a dog starts to think that maybe he is not the "leader", he starts to unwind. The stress of having to be the leader ebbs away and this can cause a dog to sleep a lot more than average.

Day 3 – A Bit of Inclusion

Start the day the same as the first two days. However, each member of the family is going to take a turn calling the dog to them. This must be done every hour, for the first five hours.

The person should command the dog to "Come". If your dog listens and comes, that person should pat him, say "Good Dog" and then leave the room. It is very essential for the *person* to walk away *first* and then go back to paying no attention to the dog.

After these first five hours, people can call the dog over at random times. If the dog comes over, that person should give the dog positive attention with words, play, pats, etc.

After five minutes, that person must turn their back and walk away. This sends an extremely forceful message to the dog about who is really in charge.

The Last Day (And Possibly Forever)

The final day will be one that sets the standard for all days in the future. For a dog that was severely aggressive, the rule for *life* will be that attention will *only* be given when a human family member initiates it. And it will end when that person wishes for it to end.

A dog can receive all the love and attention in the world! Your dog does not need to be ignored at all after the 4th day. You can take your dog for walks, play, run errands together, sit and watch TV...anything that you wish. *However, for dogs that were very aggressive, it must be the humans who begin any and all interaction.*

From Day Four and onward, any time that the dog tries to get attention, he should be completely and utterly ignored for one full minute. This reinforces the rules and helps a dog understand that the new order of the pack will not be challenged and is not negotiable: It is their human who decides when attention is given.

If this training does not work, and you wish to retain ownership of your dog, it is highly suggested to have your dog evaluated. This will be a deciding factor in regard to the future safety of all people that come into contact with your dog. When evaluating your dog *in person*, a canine behavioral specialist or canine trainer with a specialty in aggressive behavior will be able to determine any deeply hidden reasons for aggression....and if it is safe to keep the dog in the home.

Actions to Take After an Event of Actual Biting

When a dog attacks and bites someone, whether the victim is someone in your household or a stranger, there will be some difficult decisions ahead. It may be a time of unrest, as everyone has a different opinion about what to do and how to handle things. In many cases, you do not need to immediately remove your dog if you wish to keep him. However, do keep in mind that local laws *may* force a "surrender".

After a biting incident, while you are sorting things out and deciding on a course of action, it is suggested to implement the use of a basket muzzle when your dog has the potential to bite again...just until issues are resolved.

As soon as possible (within a couple of days) a full and complete medical examination should be performed by a reputable and experienced veterinarian. Not only can pain from injury or illness cause a dog to bite, there may be a neurological condition which can be detected via an MRI scan.

If all potential health issues have been ruled out, thus allowing you to know that the severe, violent aggression is *not* due to an underlying health issue, you will need to reevaluate if you wish to keep your dog. Your next choice will be to either obtain in-person intensive behavioral training or to surrender your dog.

If your dog is actually biting (and not nipping) and you are fearful for the safety of yourself or any other people, it is recommended to remove the danger; regrettably this means your dog. The safety of your human family members must come first, above all else. Dog bites can be fatal and often it is not worth the risk to try and train a dog that has been proven to actually bite.

Even if a dog has bit you one time and you were not terribly injured, *the precedence has been set* and the dog may very well bite again with much more severe consequences.

You may think that one *possible* solution is to give your dog to another person…However this is not a good idea. In many some states, it's illegal to sell or give away a dog that has bitten. In any case, you would need to live with the fact that you placed other people in potential danger. Lastly, there are people who will take a dog that has bitten in order to enter him into illegal dog fights…or to use the dog solely as a guard dog (with little human contact or care), which is an isolating and unhappy life.

Regrettably, surrendering a dog to a shelter equals a high likelihood that the dog will be put to sleep. Shelters do not re-home dogs that have been proven to bite.

If you wish to implement in-person training, it is important to know that it may or may not be successful. Much of this depends on the core character of the dog. If he has had years of experiences that led violent aggression, the best of trainers in the world may not be able to reverse this.

If you do decide to enter your dog into this type of training, you will want to limit the exposure that your dog has to any biting "triggers" and make use of the aforementioned basket muzzle while you see if training works. Once you have found an experienced trainer to work one-on-one with your dog, follow any additional advice and guidelines that he or she outlines for you.

Other books by Faye Dunningham

(Found on Amazon!)

The Well Trained Puppy: Housebreaking, Commands
to Shape Behavior and All Training Needed for a
Happy, Obedient Dog

The Well Socialized Dog: Step-by-Step Socialization
Training for Puppies and Dogs

2735169R00071

Printed in Great Britain
by Amazon.co.uk, Ltd.,
Marston Gate.